Hitchcock Becomes "HITCHCOCK"
The British Years

Hitchcock Becomes "HITCHCOCK"

The British Years

by Paul M. Jensen

Midnight Marquee Press, Inc.
Baltimore, Maryland, USA

ISBN 1-887664-88-2
Library of Congress Catalog Card Number 105414
Manufactured in the United States of America
Printed by Kirby Lithographic Company, Arlington, VA
First Printing by Midnight Marquee Press, Inc., July 2000
Second Printing, December 2008
Acknowledgments: Betty Cavanaugh, Photofest, Buddy Weiss, Linda J. Walter

To Alfred Hitchcock,
who so thoroughly shared himself with us.

Elsa (Madeleine Carroll) after the train wreck that climaxes *Secret Agent* (1936).

Table of Contents

PREFACE

Alfred Hitchcock is probably the most written about of all film directors, and his unique status surely justifies that position.

Hitchcock was prolific, having directed 53 feature films (and portions of one more). He began by making silent films, and his career extended well into the fifth decade of the sound film era. His first 23 films were made in Great Britain, after which he migrated to Hollywood, so he was highly productive in two quite different settings. Hitchcock was among the most popular of entertainers and is one of the few directors whose name became a household word. He also is the only significant and enduring link between popular entertainment and the art cinema of 1920s Germany and the Soviet Union. He sold himself like a Madison Avenue advertiser sold soap, yet he remained a remarkably personal artist as well as an expert technician with practical experience in nearly every facet of the medium.

There is no doubt about it: Alfred Hitchcock was one of a kind.

Hitchcock deserves the constant attention he still receives, for he was a complete filmmaker who provides all that a critic or audience member might seek. He is a calculating manipulator, yet he can stir the emotions by tapping into instinct and a remarkable intensity of feeling. His films reveal careful design, even as they delve into the irrational and the anarchic. He concentrates on showing concrete details, yet in the process explores ideas and themes. He offers strikingly composed individual images, but is also a master of dynamic editing. Despite his supposed disinterest in such matters, he even elicits superior performances from both respected actors and less respected movie stars.

Whenever a new film theory arises, it is tested on Hitchcock, but one also finds him featured in glossy picture books containing few critical ambitions. Somehow, Alfred Hitchcock manages to satisfy many different kinds of viewers, probably because he contained a great variety of facets within himself.

My own reactions to Hitchcock and his films have evolved over the years, and that surely is one sign of a superior director—a person whose work can seem to shift even as it remains constant, interacting with changes in the viewer's sensibility.

I discovered Hitchcock at the same time as I discovered films in general, during the mid-1950s. Also at that time I took pleasure in his television series, *Alfred Hitchcock Presents*. From then on, I followed Hitchcock's career in the present tense, while catching up with his past through television showings and 16mm screenings. Meanwhile, I developed allegiances to Orson Welles and Ingmar Bergman, to Federico Fellini and Sergei Eisenstein, to Carl Dreyer and Akira Kurosawa. Perhaps inevitably, my estimation of Hitchcock rose and fell, then rose again.

As a teacher of film at the State University of New York at Oneonta, I frequently show and discuss Hitchcock's films in my classes, and on two occasions I devoted an entire semester to his career in a Special Topics course. The process of selecting the films, viewing them with an audience, and discussing them in class is the kind of activity that makes my profession so satisfying.

This volume originated as an essay about *Rich and Strange*, which I began writing at the invitation of Gary and Sue Svehla. It is they who I must thank for the opportunity to voice my thoughts about Hitchcock and his films, thereby propelling me into the floodwaters of Hitchcock criticism.

Because I consider *Rich and Strange* a pivotal work in Hitchcock's career, dealing with that film required that I explain what came before and what followed. Ultimately, this meant discussing Hitchcock's 13 previous features as well as those he made immediately afterward, and so the essay grew into the present volume. In it, my aim has not been to provide complete analyses of these films, except *Rich and Strange*, but rather to explore the thematic and stylistic qualities that link Hitchcock's early films with his first thrillers.

Most writers on Hitchcock concentrate on his American films. Of the ones who deal with his British career, few pay much attention to the seven sound films he made before *The Man Who Knew Too Much* (1934) or to his nine silent features. Nonetheless, those 16 films comprise a substantial and rewarding body of work.

In discussing these films, I tend to mention screenwriters less often than some screenwriters might wish. There is a reason for this.

Hitchcock began as a scenario writer and he has writing credits on seven of his own films; his wife and collaborator, Alma Reville, has credits on 12. But whether or not Hitchcock is credited as a writer, he always had a significant influence on the script's or scenario's creation and evolution. "The difficulty of writing a motion picture story," Hitchcock wrote in a 1937 essay, "is to make things not only logical but visual.... It is no use telling people; they have got to SEE."[1] Because of the extent to which small actions, gestures, and objects are significant elements in Hitchcock's method of expression, he could not simply take someone else's script and film it. He, the director, had to be involved all along, helping to design the scenes and situations in order to integrate his cinematic form with the story's content.

So, without intending to slight the important contribution writers made to the finished product, the fact remains that they were Hitchcock's collaborators and their efforts reflect his needs and desires.

Hitchcock directed 24 feature films during 1925-39, of which I was able to view all but *The Pleasure Garden*, *The Mountain Eagle* (which no longer exists), *Downhill*, and *Waltzes from Vienna*. My conclusions about these four works rely primarily on the detailed descriptions provided in Maurice Yacowar's insightful and unusually accurate volume, *Hitchcock's British Films*.[2] The only relevant film not discussed in this volume is *Elstree Calling*, a musical-comedy revue with several directors and to which Hitchcock contributed little.

My thanks go to Sue and Gary Svehla, of Midnight Marquee Press, for their support and encouragement, as well as their energy.

I also wish to thank three people who read this manuscript in its various stages, and were even willing to re-read it as it evolved. Barbara Dobkowski offered useful responses throughout the work's gestation, and Mark A. Miller contributed helpful suggestions and needed encouragement. Meanwhile, Arthur Lennig offered a great deal of constructive advice, as well as constant energizing.

In addition, I am grateful to the interlibrary loan staff at SUNY-Oneonta's Milne Library, without whose service I could never have read the novels on which *Young and Innocent* and *The Lady Vanishes* were based.

INTRODUCTION

"I think you'll find that the real start of my career
was *The Man Who Knew Too Much*."
—Alfred Hitchcock to
Charles Thomas Samuels, 1972

Alfred Hitchcock's comments in his frequent interviews have encouraged many critics to assume that the director's true career began in 1934 with *The Man Who Knew Too Much*, the first in a long, almost unbroken string of thrillers. Then, having defined Hitchcock as a specialist, these critics select from his earlier work only those films that anticipate his later career: *The Lodger* (1927), *Blackmail* (1929), *Murder!* (1930), and *Number Seventeen* (1932). Such a perspective, mired in the confidence of hindsight, results in a highly misleading view of the director, one that dismisses his 12 other early features—eight silent and four sound—and implies that he was merely marking time until his "true" creative personality emerged.

The films themselves indicate otherwise. Hitchcock was, in fact, a major director from the very start of his career in 1925 and for 10 years he made substantial, mature features that reveal an impressive consistency in content and form. In addition, even such early comedies and romantic dramas as *Easy Virtue* (1927), *The Farmer's Wife* (1928), and *Champagne* (1928) have far more in common with the later thrillers than one might expect.

True, a major shift in Hitchcock's emphasis and attitude did occur in the early 1930s. The crucial moment, however, relates not to *The Man Who Knew Too Much* but to *Rich and Strange* (1932), which could be considered the single most meaningful work in his entire career.

Flush with confidence as the most successful and respected director in Britain, Hitchcock both directed and co-wrote the serio-comic *Rich and Strange*. In it, an office worker, bored with his repetitious and insignificant existence, convinces his wife to join him in an attempt to discover life. Starting as a lively satire, the film introduces romantic

A worried father (Leslie Banks) confronts a ruthless anarchist (Peter Lorre) in
***The Man Who Knew Too Much* (1934).**

complications for the couple, builds to a dramatic confrontation, then climaxes with some grim adventures. These events are much more disorienting and distressing than the main character anticipated and yet, after returning home, he seems hardly to have changed at all.

Rich and Strange summarized the interests and approaches Hitchcock had developed in 14 prior features and that he would continue exploring in his future work. At the same time, it unexpectedly marked the end of a major creative period and prompted this eclectic artist-entertainer to evolve into a thriller specialist. It clearly is a Hitchcock film, yet in many ways it differs from all his other works.

The critical and box-office failure of *Rich and Strange* left Hitchcock, like his film's character, disoriented and distressed. Having exposed his thoughts and feelings in a highly personal way, he must have felt embarrassed, even humiliated, at the double rejection. Professionally, it left him uncertain and insecure.

Not long after *Rich and Strange*, Hitchcock made *The Man Who Knew Too Much*, which was the first in a series of suspense melodramas that continued through his move to Hollywood in 1939 and until his last film in 1976. It is easy—too easy—to view these thrillers as representing a "new" Hitchcock or a "compromised" Hitchcock or the "real" Hitchcock. What they do represent is a more defensive version of the original Hitchcock.

Alfred Hitchcock on location filming *The Mountain Eagle* **(1926).**

CHAPTER ONE

HITCHCOCK DEFINED

"When moving pictures are really
artistic they will be created
entirely by one man."
— Alfred Hitchcock
London Evening News, 1927

By the end of his first two years as a director, Alfred Hitchcock had already defined himself as three men, all of whom continued, for the rest of his life, to co-exist somewhat uneasily within his ample body. From the start, he was a practical technician and craftsman who entertained audiences by telling stories clearly and efficiently. At the same time, he was an artist entranced with using film to express his characters' feelings and to stir those of his viewers, and who drew upon his own life and feelings in the process. He also was a businessman who was fully aware of the precarious nature of his position, which often depended on the whims of shallow, sometimes ruthless executives.

A major influence on Hitchcock was the American style of film production. While still in his early teens, he began reading movie trade papers and soon realized why American films were better photographed than British ones.

> I had noticed, for instance, that the Americans always tried to separate the image from the background with backlights, whereas in the British films the image melted into the background. There was no separation, no relief.[1]

In November 1927, Hitchcock wrote to the *London Evening News* that:

> American film directors under their commercially minded employers have learnt a good deal about studio lighting, action photographs, and telling a story plainly and smoothly in moving pictures.

Although Hitchcock developed an interest in filmmaking during his teens, he never sought employment with a British firm. Instead, when the American company Famous Players-Lasky (later known as Paramount) established a British studio in 1919, the young man applied for a job and was hired to design the drawings used as backgrounds for the films' intertitles. At Famous Players-Lasky, Hitchcock gained an education in cinematic principles. For example, he noticed how easily one could alter the implied meaning of a scene simply by re-writing the title cards or shifting the order of events. As he recalled:

> One could really do anything—take the end of a picture and put it at the beginning—anything at all![2]

When, in 1922, the Americans closed their London studio, the English producer Michael Balcon leased space there and retained

Hitchcock to assist his director, Graham Cutts. Soon, Hitchcock added set design and scenario writing to his other duties.

Contact with the technical skills of these pragmatic Americans was supplemented by exposure to the more artistic approach of contemporary German directors. *The Blackguard* (1925),

Staircase set designed by Hitchcock for *The Blackguard*.

The Last Laugh became a textbook of expressive filmmaking for Hitchcock.

the fifth feature for which Hitchcock wrote the scenario, designed the sets, and served as Cutts's assistant, was a co-production with Ufa, the German company. As part of this arrangement, the film was shot at Ufa's Berlin studio, where major directors were creating highly visual and atmospheric films. Hitchcock, in order to build one of his sets, had to tear down the imposing forest constructed for Fritz Lang's recently completed *Siegfrieds Tod* (*Siegfried's Death*; Part I of *Die Nibelungen*, 1924).

More significantly, Hitchcock visited a neighboring set, where F.W. Murnau was directing *Der letzte Mann* (*The Last Man*, a.k.a. *The Last Laugh*, 1924), a picture that for Hitchcock became a virtual textbook of expressive filmmaking. He may already have been thinking along similar lines, but Murnau's classic offered the young man a brilliant lesson in the use of pure cinema to tell a story and to reveal a character's thoughts and feelings. It was, Hitchcock said decades later:

> ...almost the perfect film. It told its story even without subtitles — from beginning to end entirely by the use

of imagery, and that had a tremendous influence on me.[3]

Hitchcock was especially taken by Murnau's use of editing to show what his central character sees, which lets viewers follow the man's train of thought and, thereby, understand how he feels. At times, Murnau also employed special lenses, which distorted the look of external reality to convey the character's inner state. Thus, by purely visual means, Murnau admitted viewers into the character's mind and emotions. For example, after the main character has been demoted from his job as a hotel doorman, he tries to hide the news from his friends by stealing the impressive uniform. Here, Murnau conveys the man's feeling of hopelessness by having the hotel appear to tilt forward, as if collapsing on top of him. On another occasion, the character's inebriation is shown through subjective shots that split one figure into three.

Watching Murnau at work was a watershed experience for Hitchcock, and upon returning to England he supplemented his first-hand knowledge through the screenings of the London Film Society. Formed by a group of film enthusiasts in 1925, this organization arranged private showings of movies seldom booked into British theaters. The Film Society emphasized the art of the medium and often screened recent works by German, Russian, and French directors who experimented with style and content. Hitchcock was a member from virtually the beginning.

Thus, Hitchcock saw himself as both a storyteller and an artist: He accepted the commercial nature of movie making, but he also loved using film expressively. Hitchcock voiced this dichotomy when, in 1927, he referred to the need to use

> ...the nouns, verbs, and adjectives of the film language.... as cunningly as do the great novelist and the great dramatist, to achieve certain moods and effects on an audience.

However, he added:

> We must not forget that our duty is always to provide entertainment for those who pay.[4]

Although in 1927 Hitchcock was already an established director, he had grasped these matters even before making his own first feature.

The third facet of Hitchcock-the-director also took form at the start of his career, when he learned just how unstable the business could be. Graham Cutts, noting the young man's abilities and the attention they were receiving, tried to sabotage Hitchcock by telling the studio's head, Michael Balcon, that he no longer wanted him as an assistant. Hitchcock recalled:

> I was maneuvered deliberately away from my job and I knew who it was and how it was done. It happens in our business all the time.[5]

Although Balcon acceded to Cutts's demand, the ploy backfired because Balcon then did the unexpected: He made Hitchcock a director, thereby placing the 25-year-old on the same level as Cutts.

The first two films directed by Hitchcock, *The Pleasure Garden* and *The Mountain Eagle*, were British-German co-productions shot on location in Europe and in a Munich studio during the summer and fall of 1925. When Hitchcock returned to London in January 1926, he was disturbed to find little

On location for *The Mountain Eagle*

ARTLEE PICTURES CORPORATION

Arthur A. Lee, president, presents

The Pleasure Garden

FROM THE PUBLISHED BOOK BY OLIVER SANDYS

WITH VIRGINIA VALLI & CARMELITA GERAGHTY

Directed by Alfred Hitchcock

A GAINSBOROUGH PICTURE

In *The Lodger* (1926), the intentions of the title character (Ivor Novello) toward Daisy (June) may not be what they seem.

enthusiasm for the release of either production. *The Pleasure Garden* finally received a trade screening in March 1926, but C.M. Woolf, who distributed Balcon's films, decided that the picture would confuse audiences and ordered it shelved, even though *The Bioscope* called it "a film of outstanding merit" and *Picturegoer* praised Hitchcock's "complete grasp of all the different branches of film technique."[6]

It was in this unsettled atmosphere of critical praise and studio resistance that Hitchcock shot *The Lodger* for the same company during the summer of 1926. In his autobiography, Michael Balcon explained that Graham Cutts

> ...began to tell anybody who would listen that we had a disaster on our hands. Unfortunately one person who listened

In this staged behind-the-scenes shot for *The Mountain Eagle*, Hitchcock directs, with Alma Reville in support.

to him was C.M. Woolf, who, of course, had the say as to distribution.[7]

When Woolf called *The Lodger* incomprehensible and refused to release it, Balcon hired Hitchcock's friend Ivor Montagu, a founding member of the Film Society, to revise the film. A modified version was shown to the trade in September, and The Bioscope's review declared, "It is possible that this film is the finest British production ever made." A trade screening of *The Mountain Eagle* followed, which prompted The Bioscope to refer to Hitchcock's "skillful, and at times brilliant direction."[8]

The Pleasure Garden finally reached London theaters in January 1927, with *The Lodger* following in February and *The Mountain*

Eagle in May. By this time, Hitchcock's fourth film, *Downhill*, was being screened for the trade press and *Kinematograph Weekly* called it "another personal success" for Hitchcock, while *The Bioscope* declared that "the selling angle is the name of Hitchcock."[9] *Easy Virtue* (1927), based on a play by Noel Coward, then completed Hitchcock's contract with Balcon. It was now clear—despite the efforts of Cutts and Woolf—that Hitchcock's films satisfied audiences instead of confusing them.

This happy ending came about mainly because of the critical praise received by the films and by Hitchcock himself. The critics had helped to get Hitchcock's films before the public, to make his name widely known, and to place him at the forefront of the British industry. The young director recognized this and, one day in 1926, he declared to some Film Society friends that movies should be made not for the distributors or even for the public, but for the press. According to his authorized biographer, John Russell Taylor, Hitchcock explained that critics

> ...were the only ones who could give one freedom—direct the public what to see, hold a gun at the heads of the distributors and exhibitors. If you could keep in well with them, keep your name and work in the papers, and so the public eye, the rest was easy.[10]

The complex history of his first three films gave Hitchcock good reason not to have confidence in conservative businessmen such as C.M. Woolf. Instead, he chose to cultivate the critics through personal publicity, which he saw as the only way to obtain influence and independence. Revealingly, by this time Hitchcock had already created the sketch of his profile that helped popularize his identity. In 1927, the results were obvious. Upon leaving Balcon, Hitchcock joined the newly formed British International Pictures at a salary of more than three times what Balcon had paid.[11]

In *Champagne* (1928), the heroine (Betty Balfour) believes her father to be ruined financially, so she looks for a job in show business.

Hitchcock's first film for B.I.P., *The Ring* (1927), won over the critics—*The Bioscope* called it "the most magnificent British film ever made" [12]—but it was not a box office success, so Hitchcock followed it with two romantic comedies, *The Farmer's Wife* (1928) and *Champagne* (1928). His final silent film, *The Manxman* (1929), was called by *The Bioscope* a film of "remarkable power and gripping interest,"[13] and audiences also responded favorably.

On the verge of making the transition to sound films, Hitchcock had achieved what he had sought: a relatively stable and secure position in an unstable, insecure business. He was praised, he was respected, and he was bankable. What is more, he had gained that status without lowering his artistic standards. He was, in fact, doing what every artist must do—exercising his creative imagination in the medium of his choice, using subjects and situations that were personally meaningful. And he did so while seeming to be merely an entertainer.

To English-speaking critics and audiences of the time, "art" announced its seriousness and its meaning overtly. Hitchcock, however, was drawn to the Continental manner, to what he called "the oblique approach,"[14] which conveys meaning indirectly, through suggestion. Thus, while a film's story elements—events, characterizations, settings, objects—exist as concrete facts and can be appreciated solely on that level, they also function metaphorically. Hitchcock was attracted to this approach from the start. In his first film job, he drew pictures to accompany the words on title cards and, as he explained it:

> ...if the line read: "George was leading a very fast life by this time," I would draw a candle, with a flame at each end, just below the sentence.[15]

As a director, Hitchcock did much the same thing, using concrete, visual images to embody abstract concepts.

This style forces viewers to register details and draw conclusions from them, which is what Hitchcock, in a 1939 lecture at New York's Columbia University, called "keeping the mind of the spectator occupied." However, he did not necessarily expect viewers to analyze the content of his images. On the contrary, the process is less conscious and intellectual than instinctive. As Hitchcock wrote in his 1965 *Encyclopaedia Britannica* entry on film production, "The impact of the image is directly on emotions."

The victimizer has become the victim in *Blackmail* (1929).

CHAPTER TWO
A VISUAL LANGUAGE

"Everything in cinema is a visual statement
and the images are its language."
—Alfred Hitchcock[1]

It was already evident in his earliest films that the basis of Hitchcock's art is vision. This emphasis has its origin in the director's personality, as it evolved in childhood. He recalled in 1962:

> At family gatherings I would sit quietly
> in a corner, saying nothing. I looked
> and observed a good deal. I've always
> been that way and still am.[2]

As a result, his films are defined by a process of guided observation, in which Hitchcock—through careful selection of what to show and how to show it—leads viewers to draw certain conclusions about his characters and situations.

This manner of expression, like so much in Hitchcock's style, reveals the influence of Murnau's *Der letzte Mann*. For example, in that film, the main character's descent from doorman to bathroom attendant is represented by the sight of him disappearing down a flight of stairs into darkness, as glass doors swing shut in the foreground, cutting him off from the world above. In *Downhill*, Hitchcock does almost the same thing when he has a character start his moral decline by descending out of view on an escalator. The events in Hitchcock's films often serve this kind of double duty,

**Roddy (Ivor Novello) is wrongly accused of a sexual indiscretion in *Downhill*
(1927).**

developing the physical action of the plot while also conveying,
through implication, the inner psychological or emotional
elements.

That this is a conscious aspect of Hitchcock's style can be seen
from *The Ring*, which was based on Hitchcock's original scenario.
In this plot, the events thoroughly embody the characters' feelings
and relationships. "One Round" Jack Sander (Carl Brisson), a
boxer, is engaged to the woman (Lilian Hall-Davis) who sells
tickets at the fairground concession where he meets all comers.
When Bob Corby (Ian Hunter) reveals an interest in the woman,
Jack challenges him, but Bob accepts only after the woman
questions his ability (hence, his virility). Bob turns out to be a top
professional boxer and he defeats Jack, after which the woman

"One Round" Jack Sander (Carl Brisson), flanked by his trainer (Gordon Harker) and a sideshow barker (Harry Terry), in *The Ring* (1927).

reveals, "We were hoping to get married, and now you've probably lost him his job!" So Bob hires Jack, which keeps the woman in his orbit, although to Jack the steady income means only that he and the woman can finally marry.

Their wedding, however, does not end the flirtation and the woman seems to pay more attention to Bob than to her husband. Thus, the fact that Jack works as Bob's sparring partner embodies the men's complex personal relationship, which combines partnership with rivalry. Finally, Jack declares, "It seems as though I shall have to fight for my wife after all," and works his way up in the standings until matched with Bob for the championship. Thus, a public event—the climactic fight—resolves the men's conflict. For *The Ring*, Hitchcock created a plot that serves as a prolonged metaphor, with the men supporting and challenging each other in two parallel ways: professionally and personally.

The scenarios for Hitchcock's eight other silent films are credited to Eliot Stannard, but it can be assumed that Hitchcock—who had written five scenarios before turning director—exerted considerable influence on the results, because in each case external situations frequently embody the characters' inner, emotional states.

For example, a scene early in *The Manxman* indirectly reveals the relationship of the three main characters. "I'm off to foreign parts to make my fortune," Pete Quilliam (Carl Brisson) tells Kate Creegeen (Anny Ondra) through her second floor bedroom window. When he asks her to wait for him, she hesitates, then agrees. However, Pete can reach Kate's window only by standing on the shoulders of his friend, Philip Christian (Malcolm Keen). Thus, the physical situation embodies the emotional one, as Pete relies on his friend for support and Philip defers to Pete's love for Kate, despite his own interest in her.

At times, Hitchcock's choices offer subtle overtones that become clear only as the film progresses. In *Easy Virtue*, the heroine telephones her response to a marriage proposal and the switchboard operator reveals the answer through her facial expressions, which shift from concern and disappointment to pleasure and relief. Initially, this seems only a charming, typically Hitchcockian use of indirection. In retrospect, though, the operator's reactions turn ironic, because she naïvely assumes that a "yes" will result in happiness for the couple.

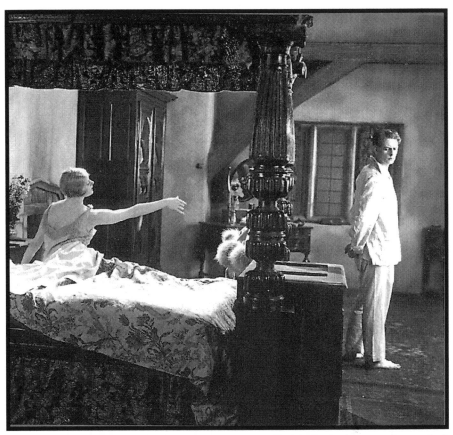

Larita Filton (Isabel Jeans) and John Whittaker (Robin Irvine) are a mismatched married couple in *Easy Virtue* (1927).

A comparable situation occurs in *The Ring*, during another marriage proposal: When Jack and his fiancée seal their engagement with a kiss, Hitchcock does not show the moment directly. Instead, we see it as a reflection in the rippling surface of a lake, an image that is as unstable as their present commitment and their future life together. Unlike the telephone operator scene, however, this shot's impact derives from how Hitchcock shows the action, not from the action itself. Similarly, in *The Manxman*, during the celebration of Kate's marriage to Pete, Hitchcock composes a shot of the newlyweds separated by their tall wedding cake, which hints at the truth beneath this seemingly happy scene. Because Hitchcock relied on such expressive visual devices, the writing of his films was inseparable from his direction.

The opening of *The Farmer's Wife* is a calculatedly elliptical sequence that clearly illustrates how Hitchcock could control his viewers' perceptions. A workman (Gordon Harker) is shown entering a farmhouse, while another man (Jameson Thomas) gazes out through an upstairs window. After some pastoral shots of the farm and its animals, two puppies enter the house and climb the stairs. The workman emerges from an upstairs room and descends, ignoring the dogs, as the other man continues to look out the window. Once outside, the workman glances up and the other man shakes his head, then the workman moves on. So far, these images have been very precise, but from them viewers can glean only a mood of sorrow and tension; we do not know who these people are or what is occurring in the upstairs room.

At this point, the man at the window turns and Hitchcock finally shows the room's interior: The man looks toward three women who are gathered at another woman's bedside. In a medium shot, the bedridden woman sits up and says to one of the others, "Don't forget to air your master's pants, 'Minta." She then lies down, leaving 'Minta (Lilian Hall-Davis) alone in the shot. In the same frame, the shadow of a hand appears on a wall and pulls a curtain closed, darkening the room and ending the scene. This visually compact, emotionally sensitive shot suggests the death of the farmer's wife, while the entire sequence delicately evokes a mood of passive, sad anticipation. The dialogue title card (the only intertitle in the film's first seven minutes) puts most of what we have seen in perspective, while identifying the scene's three main characters and their relationships.

Because Hitchcock has shown these events without establishing a context for them, the viewer's attention is caught, even as the action proceeds, with a confident precision that reassures while it temporarily bewilders. This sequence is not a flashy cinematic stunt. Rather it epitomizes Hitchcock's belief that form is more important than content. If directed in a standard, straightforward fashion—the way most directors worked—the scene would have functioned as a declarative sentence, a statement of facts, and our sense of its significance would depend on the significance those

Farmer Sweetland (Jameson Thomas) can not believe his proposal has been rejected by Mary Hearn (Olga Slade) in *The Farmer's Wife* (1928).

facts hold for us. Hitchcock, however, uses form to involve viewers with the situation's inner meaning: He shows only concrete details, but he communicates the intangible. Thus, when Hitchcock says that he has no interest in "content," it should not be assumed that he has no interest in meaning.

This sequence is rather unusual, even for Hitchcock, but in less extreme ways he frequently uses film technique to link viewers with a character and to provide information and insight. He does this by using shots that force viewers to share the character's vision, by showing what that person sees from his or her point of view. In *The Farmer's Wife*, after the daughter of the widower, Samuel Sweetland, has been married, a meal is served at his house. During it, someone says, "There be many here who have oft been wishful of a partner." Sweetland smiles, then his expression becomes serious. As Sweetland looks to his right, Hitchcock cuts to what the man sees, an empty chair. From this, the audience understands Sweetland's sense of his late wife's absence. However, because viewers aren't "told" this, but draw it as a conclusion based on what is seen, they are forced to be "inside" the character's feeling and, therefore, are more likely to share it.

At another point during the meal, the laughing bride looks up and her smile fades. Why? Because she sees her father looking morose. Then, he glances up at her, smiles, and nods. She is relieved. Here, Hitchcock charts a subtle emotional exchange between father and daughter, showing us what lies just below the scene's surface action.

Later, after the newlyweds and guests have gone, Sweetland stands alone, brushes confetti from his jacket, and toys with

 some that he holds in his hand. This prompts him to look up at his own wedding picture, then down at the empty chair. He sits, still gazing at the chair opposite, as light from the fireplace flickers like memories on his face. Soon he rises again, pauses to think, then goes to a mirror where he examines his reflection and brushes his

Hitchcock relies on what Sweetland sees in the mirror to tell the audience what he is thinking in *The Farmer's Wife.*

mustache. Here, Hitchcock's sensitive editing allows us to enter Sweetland's thoughts, his feelings, and his decision to seek a new wife. Hitchcock does this by showing what Sweetland looks at, and those objects' associations—not the objects themselves—reveal what is in his mind and, by extension, how he feels.

Throughout his career, Hitchcock relied on shots of what a character sees, but in his silent films he frequently went further. Instead of showing what the person literally sees, and what anyone standing in that spot would see, Hitchcock manipulates the image so that we perceive what the person thinks, recalls, or imagines. This usually involves modifying the appearance of reality to convey a psychological or emotional truth. Often, he uses superimpositions to create multiple images, with the separate elements replacing and combining with each other; at times, a distorting lens further alters the image. Thus, we share not just a point of view, but a subjective mental state.

An example occurs in *The Farmer's Wife* when Sweetland considers three marriage prospects. As he imagines them replacing his late wife, he looks at her empty chair and each woman's image dissolves into the shot and the chair, then out again. Virtually all of Hitchcock's early films contain moments like this, which conjure up a character's thoughts. In *The Ring*, an important boxing match is shown through images superimposed on the face of Jack's fiancée, who is not present; what we receive, then, is the fight as she imagines it, not as it really occurs. Similarly, in *The Manxman*, Hitchcock personalizes Kate's wedding—renders it subjective— by superimposing the details over a close-up of her face during the ceremony.

In *Easy Virtue*, Hitchcock combines this technique with others to develop the fact that Larita Filton (Isabel Jeans) is haunted by her reputation, which was damaged at her first divorce when the jury found her "guilty of misconduct." The title card that announces this verdict includes the image of a newspaper reporter's camera. This immediately links the court's findings with publicity (using a visual device Hitchcock had developed in his first cinema job). Then, as Larita leaves the courtroom, she shies away from several press photographers. Seeking to escape this kind of attention, she travels to the French Riviera and, when she starts to sign the hotel register with her real name, a subjective shot of the page dissolves to a close-up of a camera pointing at us (and at her). After a moment's thought, Larita writes her last name as Gray, anticipating Hitchcock's 1962 comment that

> ...villains are not all black and heroes
> are not all white; there are grays
> everywhere.[3]

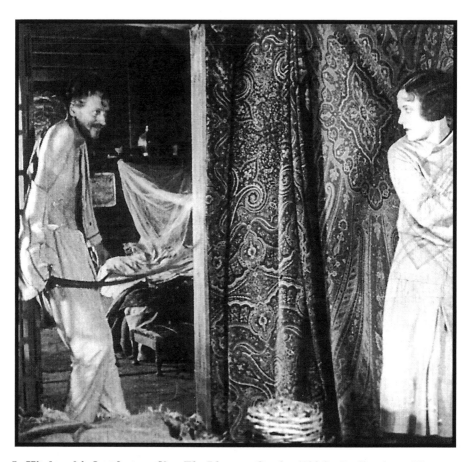

In Hitchcock's first feature film, *The Pleasure Garden* (1926), the disoriented Levett (Miles Mander) attacks the heroine Patsy (Virginia Valli). (Photofest)

Later, after she marries a young man (Robin Irvine) ignorant of her past, Larita realizes that his family knows her ex-husband's attorney. Retreating to the living room, she reveals her fear when she sees a camera resting on a table and knocks it off. Ultimately, a magazine photograph reveals her secret to the family and, after a second divorce, the film ends as Larita again faces press photographers outside a courthouse. (Ironically, while directing this film about the negative power of publicity, Hitchcock was himself attempting to cultivate and control the power of the press.)

Hitchcock's most dramatic use of subjective vision occurs when a character becomes disoriented. This happens about once per film, starting with his first picture, *The Pleasure Garden*, in which a feverish man drowns his mistress, then sees her demanding that he kill his wife. Hitchcock uses special lenses to make viewers share the distorted vision of an inebriated man in *The Ring* and a seasick man in *Champagne*. Later in *Champagne*, the heroine is told by her millionaire father that he is ruined and Hitchcock evokes the impact of the news by superimposing a shot of the whirling room over her face.

A more elaborate version of this technique appears in *The Ring*. While Jack talks business with a fight promoter, his wife attends a party in the next room and, through a mirror reflection, Jack sees her sitting on the arm of his rival's chair. Then, in a subjective shot, the camera observes the men talking to Jack, but the couple's image is superimposed over their figures. As Jack's suspicion grows, the music from the party becomes distorted in his mind, which Hitchcock conveys through a multiple image of a phonograph record and hands playing instruments. The tension builds within Jack, until he finally pictures the couple kissing and explodes with anger at what he imagines is happening.

This use of visual style is not just a way to convey information or to keep viewers interested by linking them with a character. Its implications extend much further, into the plots and characterizations. Over and over, in Hitchcock's films, people draw conclusions and make judgments based on what they see, which they assume (often erroneously) to be true. At times, the film's viewers are placed in the same situation.

The Lodger is the first Hitchcock film constructed around this concept of faulty vision and misinterpretation. Because there is a killer of blonde women at large, from the moment the mysterious lodger (Ivor Novello) appears from out of nowhere to rent a room in the home of the blonde Daisy (June) and her family, he inspires suspicion, especially when he shows an interest in Daisy. The film's audience and most of its characters deduce that this interest is menacing, when in fact it is protective.

Several specific situations develop this concept of misjudgment. At one point Joe (Malcolm Keen), a policeman who is courting

French poster for *The Lodger*

Daisy, hears a scream and rushes in to find her in the lodger's arms. Joe's (and the viewer's) two assumptions—that she is in danger and that they are embracing—are both wrong, for she was just scared by a mouse. Later, the men's roles are reversed when the lodger sees Joe wrestling with Daisy in a seemingly threatening way. (Although their tussle is playful, in a deeper sense the false impression is correct, because Joe is not a good match for Daisy and is, therefore, a threat to her welfare.) On another occasion, while Daisy and the lodger play chess, Hitchcock shows the man's actions—such as reaching for a fireplace poker—in ways that make the audience misjudge his intentions.

Much about *The Lodger* evokes Hitchcock's later thrillers, but during the 1920s its theme and technique also turn up in such non-thrillers as *Easy Virtue*. When that film starts, the judge at Larita's divorce hearing raises his monocle so he can see her better, with Hitchcock implying that the court's vision is not as clear as it should be. In a flashback, representing Larita's testimony, we see her resist the embrace of an artist who has been painting her portrait. Then, when her husband enters, we recognize how compromising their position looks to him and we understand his jealousy. In only a few shots, Hitchcock adroitly reveals the truth, while also conveying how the facts can be misinterpreted. Reacting like the husband, the jury itself makes assumptions based on appearances. As one over-confident juror explains, "The attractive wife of a drunken husband—alone all day with another man who loved her—the evidence looks conclusive to me."

During the rest of *Easy Virtue*, life itself functions like a courtroom, with people's judgments affected by faulty vision or an incomplete perception of facts. As Larita and John Whittaker ride in a carriage on the Riviera, she mentions the view, and the infatuated youth replies, "I'm afraid I've no eyes for anything but you." This seemingly romantic statement contains the seed of their future problems, for John's vision is so limited that, although he thinks he knows Larita and thinks he loves her, he is wrong on both points.

After John marries Larita and brings her to meet his family, *Easy Virtue* becomes a mirror reflection of *The Lodger*. In both films, a mysterious stranger enters a domestic setting, inspiring affection in one family member and suspicion in others. This time, though, the intruder is female and the viewers share her perspective instead of the family's. The outcome also differs: Larita is "exposed" as undesirable, whereas the lodger turns out to be rich and eligible. In a similar reversal, Daisy was the only person who saw the lodger clearly, whereas John's commitment to Larita is so undermined by his mother's skepticism that, when he learns about her past, he misjudges her as wrongly in a negative way as he had, earlier, in a positive way. The contexts of *The Lodger* and *Easy Virtue* may be totally different, but in both films a person's life is controlled by reputation—an impression created by false perceptions.

In *Downhill*, made between these films, Roddy (Ivor Novello) is blamed for a friend's sexual indiscretion and even his father assumes that he is guilty. At one point, Hitchcock ingeniously uses film technique to involve the viewer in the unstable process of drawing accurate conclusions from vis-ual evidence. After Roddy leaves home, the next scene begins (as described by John Russell Taylor) with him "looking reasonably cheerful, in evening dress. Then the camera pulls back and we realize that he is in fact a waiter. The couple he is waiting on then get up from the table and move on to the dance floor, where they seem to be performing with slightly surprising abandon." As the camera reveals more, "the 'waiter' joins in the dance also, and we are able now to see that this is all taking place on a stage, before an audience as part of a musical comedy."[4] Under Hitchcock's guidance, the film viewer's range of vision keeps changing, which alters the evidence at hand and prompts a series of conclusions, all but the last of which is undermined.

Hitchcock uses editing to accomplish something similar in *Champagne*. A major supporting character is an urbane man (Theo von Alten) who seems determined to seduce the heroine (Betty

When he finds the heroine (Betty Balfour) working in a cabaret, her boyfriend (Jean Bradin) misunderstands and becomes jealous in *Champagne*.

Balfour), an assumption made by both the girl and the viewers. At a nightclub, he lures her from their table to a private alcove, where

Anny Ondra as Kate Cregeen, the long-suffering heroine of Hitchcock's last silent film *The Manxman* **(1929). (Photofest)**

he attacks her and she runs out, screaming. Then, Hitchcock cuts to the girl still sitting with him at the table. Only now do we realize that the melodramatic events of the previous two minutes were the playing out of what she expects will happen, based on her (false) interpretation of the man's manner.

To the heroine of *Champagne*, little in life is what it appears to be. She believes her millionaire father (Gordon Harker) when he states that they are ruined, but he is lying to teach his self-indulgent daughter a lesson, and the man she perceives as a seducer is merely someone the father asked to protect her from fortune hunters. Like this woman, Jack Sander in *The Ring* suffers from a failure to "see" clearly when he does not realize that Bob Corby is flirting with his girl and that she is drawn to him. Samuel Sweetland in *The Farmer's Wife* is also blind to the world around him, as he courts four none-too-appealing ladies, and only at the end realizes that his attractive, efficient, and adoring housekeeper is the ideal choice.

The characters in *The Manxman* also misjudge both events and people. After falling in love with his friend's fiancée, Philip learns of Pete's death at sea. Kate seems to have taken the news hard. "She hasn't spoken a word since the news came," says her father. Philip approaches Kate, who stands alone, with her back turned. Expecting to console her, he is shocked and disturbed when she turns and says, "We're free." Philip and Kate's father and the audience have all misinterpreted her manner.

Kate may seem callous here, but she is just being honest. Later, when Pete returns, she insists on telling him the truth, but Philip, who earlier had seemed sincere, reveals his weakness by refusing. When Pete enters, he realizes that Kate is pregnant, but falsely—and joyously—assumes the baby is his. Philip then tells Kate, "He must never know the real truth" (as if another kind of truth exists). Kate marries Pete, but because she cannot endure a life of deceit she leaves him. When Kate returns for the baby, Pete mistakenly thinks she has come back to him and welcomes her. Told that the child is not his, he cries out, "A lie!" He's wrong, literally, but because he has lovingly tended the child, in a sense the baby *is* more his than Philip's. The film's climax takes place in a courtroom, where Philip is the judge and Kate is unexpectedly brought in, a case of attempted suicide. Her father, glancing back and forth at the two, finally realizes the truth and exposes Philip as Kate's lover. "Can't you see, Pete? Can't you see?" he asks his son-in-law, a basic question that could also have been asked of John Whittaker or Jack Sander or Samuel Sweetland.

From his youth, Hitchcock had been fond of the theater, so it is no surprise that these films often place their characters in public arenas. Showgirls perform on stage in *The Pleasure Garden* and *The Lodger*, Roddy becomes an actor and is deceived by an actress in *Downhill*, Larita is on exhibit in court and eventually plays the role her in-laws expect in *Easy Virtue*, Philip is exposed in a courtroom in *The Manxman*, and Jack Sander resolves his rivalry with Bob Corby during a boxing match in *The Ring*. Rarely, in the more extreme of these cases, does the "audience" realize

Italian lobby card for *The Pleasure Garden*

what is happening beneath the surface of these "shows." This theatrical motif serves Hitchcock well as a metaphor that echoes the more everyday forms of public observation and illusion.

Hitchcock draws attention to the act of observing and drawing conclusions—and the difficulty of doing that accurately—when, in *The Pleasure Garden*, male audience members use visual aids (binoculars, a monocle) as they watch dancers perform, which is similar to the judge in *Easy Virtue* using his monocle. At times, this process shifts from the theater to the performers' outside lives. In *The Pleasure Garden*, an audience member likes a dancer because of her blonde curl, so she removes that false decoration and hands it to him. The reverse happens in *The Lodger*: Because the murderer's victims are blonde, a fair-haired chorus girl tucks artificial black curls under her hat before leaving the theater. In *Easy Virtue*, the jury judges Larita in a public context and John's family does the same in private.

Time and time again, the way an individual is perceived by others conflicts with the "real" self. Usually, a clear vision is achieved by the film's end. However, in *The Lodger*, the title "All stories have an end" leads to an abrupt epilogue, which suggests the unlikely nature of a happy conclusion (and recalls the arbitrary happy ending of Murnau's *Der letzte Mann*). In *Easy Virtue*, we have one of Hitchcock's most uncompromising final scenes, with Larita barely holding up under the collapse of her second marriage.

CHAPTER THREE
WOMEN AND MEN

"I believe that the vast majority of
women, in all ranks of life,
are idealists."
— Alfred Hitchcock[1]

The Ring, written solely by Hitchcock, shows how the director, still in his 20s and married for less than a year, viewed a romantic relationship. At the film's beginning, Jack Sander is a winner, having knocked out every challenger, and he plans to marry the woman who assists in his public performances. After Bob Corby defeats Jack, those wedding plans are threatened, but not because the woman's commitment shifts to the other man. As she explains to Bob, "We were hoping to get married, and now you've probably lost him his job!" Soon after, Jack reveals that he might become Bob's sparring partner. "If I win the trial fight," he tells her, "we'll get married the day after." Jack does win, so he gets the job. "I'm going to make real money now," he says to his fiancée, and thus the marriage takes place.

Obviously, Jack needs professional status before he can wed. He must be a success and have the confidence that implies. This perspective reflects Hitchcock's own outlook, for he, too, waited until he became Graham Cutts's writer, designer, and assistant before courting Alma Reville, who was already an editor and had worked in the film industry longer than Hitchcock. It was "unthinkable," he recalled

> ...for a British male to admit that a woman has a more important job than his, and I waited until I had the higher position.[2]

Hitchcock and Alma on location for *The Mountain Eagle*.

By the same token, Hitchcock and Alma did not actually marry until December 2, 1926, after his first films had been taken off the shelf and his reputation established. As he explained 30 years later, "I felt the bargaining power implicit in" becoming a director "was necessary" in order to marry Alma.[3]

The Ring is told from Jack's perspective, not the woman's, so her feelings about Jack and Bob are not always clear and her actions are sometimes puzzling. Although this vagueness could be seen as a weakness, Hitchcock's approach does admit the viewer to a complex psychological and emotional situation, instead of a standard romantic triangle. The woman is not necessarily disappointed in Jack when he is defeated by Bob and becomes dependent on him for a job. She may be impressed by Bob's attentiveness to her, but she unhesitatingly marries Jack and, it can

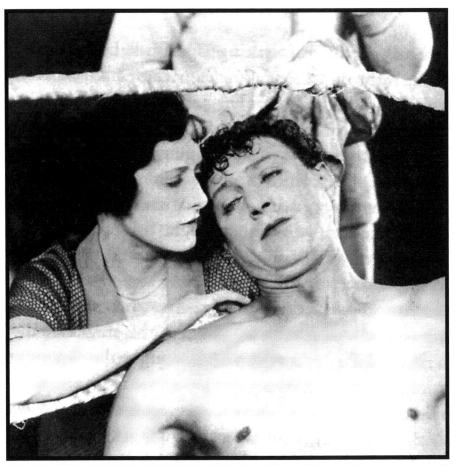

**His wife (Lilian Hall-Davis) tells Jack Sander, "I'm with you—in your corner,"
during the final fight in *The Ring*.**

be argued, she is not lured from her husband by his rival. Rather,
Jack imagines that the situation is worse than it is and his growing
jealousy drives her from him, which then seems to confirm his
suspicions.

The husband's personality is relevant, here, for although Jack
is ostensibly the "hero," he mixes innocent enthusiasm and naïveté
with smug overconfidence and, later, defensiveness. In the final
fight scene, when Jack sees his wife in the audience, he pauses
and is hit. She is distressed at this, moves to his side of the ring,
and tells him, "I'm with you—in *your* corner." This gives Jack the
needed energy and he wins. The woman seems to love Jack most

when he is least strong or dominant, and if her presence makes him vulnerable, it also motivates his achievement.

The Ring puts into perspective the courtships and marriages seen in Hitchcock's other early films. In *Easy Virtue*, for example, after Larita testifies that her husband was a cruel alcoholic and that the artist painting her portrait fell in love with her, a juror concludes, "Pity is akin to love." Later, having met and married John Whittaker, Larita illustrates that comment: Seeing John in the cocoon of his childhood home, with no psychological or emotional independence, she realizes that her initial attraction had been a semi-maternal response to his innocence and awkwardness—a form of pity.

Easy Virtue generally avoids melodramatic oversimplification, treating its characters, even the weak John, with sympathetic understanding. Mr. Whittaker, for example, accepts Larita, calling her "a very fascinating woman" and declaring that her past life "is no affair of ours." However, he is thoroughly intimidated by his wife and, therefore, ineffectual. The single exception is John's mother, whom Hitchcock seems unwilling to tolerate, to forgive, or to understand.

The personality and relationships of John Whittaker clearly

relate to those of the film's director. John's naïveté—he is inexperienced with women and doesn't even know how to mix a drink properly—recalls that of Hitchcock, who at the age of 23 had "never been out with a girl in my life" and had "never had a drink in my life."[4] In addition, Hitchcock's mother played a dominant role in his life. Donald Spoto, in his biography of the director, refers to Mrs. Hitchcock's "doting affection" for her son.[5] Hitchcock's father had died when the boy was 15, after which his mother "demanded even more attention, care, and... contact with the child who remained at home."[6] From childhood through his early years of employment, Hitchcock would stand, each evening, "at the foot of his mother's bed and answer her detailed questions about the business of the day." Spoto concludes that Hitchcock's devotion to her was the kind demanded "by a mother whose interest in her son's life imprisons rather than frees."[7] After Hitchcock married Alma, Mrs. Hitchcock often spent time with the couple, and "on these occasions he felt more compelled to satisfy her whims than to attend to his wife's comfort."[8]

Although there is no record of Mrs. Hitchcock's reaction to meeting her son's fiancée, clues can be found in the frequency with which parents in Hitchcock's films are wary of those to whom their children feel attracted. In *The Lodger*, they fear the man who intrudes on their domestic stability and who stirs Daisy's interest, and in *Champagne*, a father tries to make his daughter break up with the man who wants to marry her. In *The Manxman*, Kate's innkeeper father rejects Pete as a suitor for his daughter because he is penniless, while Philip's aunt (and surrogate mother) refers condescendingly to "that publican's daughter," warning him not to "spoil your future by a foolish entanglement." She also declares that Philip's father "married beneath him" and adds, "let his ruined career be a warning to you."

The weaknesses of the male are well documented in Hitchcock's films, but *The Manxman* puts them in clear focus. At first, Philip seems motivated by loyalty to his friend, but that is a self-deception and Philip is actually weak and selfish, concerned mainly with his own welfare. Instead of facing facts, he leaves the island. Then, when he returns, Kate reveals that she is pregnant with his child. "You kept away from me—you thought more of your future than mine," she says. Kate wants to tell Pete the truth, but Philip stalls, asking her to wait. "Think of the shame," he says, sounding like his aunt. Later, on the day Philip is to be appointed the island's judge, Kate leaves Pete and confronts her lover. "I want to be with you," she tells him, "do take me, Philip." When he hesitates, she

The dramatic landscape plays a part in *The Manxman*, as Phillip Christian (Malcolm Keen) falls in love with Kate Cregeen.

says bluntly, "The time has come when you must choose between your career and me." However, he cannot face either his love or his responsibility and urges her to "be patient," to give him more "time to think."

Of all Hitchcock's silent films, *The Farmer's Wife*, a story about courtship, provides the clearest definition of what marriage involves. In the process, it offers two seemingly inconsistent views of its main character, a widower. During the early scenes, set in his home, Samuel Sweetland is reserved and dignified, a figure of sensitivity and calm confidence. However, when he leaves the security of his farm, a totally different man emerges, a foolish incompetent totally lacking in dignity. Preparing to embark on a courtship, he smugly declares that the woman "will come like a lamb to the slaughter." He has, however, a false notion of his own appeal. Clumsy and undiplomatic, he tells the prospective bride, "You're the first to know your good luck, my dear."

Not only is Sweetland unaware of his incompetence in courtship, but he is blind to his housekeeper's love for him and his dependence on her. Araminta is efficient and caring, deferential and tolerant, but he takes her ministrations for granted. At times, he is even grumpy and irritable with her. When Sweetland departs to visit his fourth prospect, Hitchcock's camera holds on 'Minta as she watches him leave, but by now a viewer is hard pressed to recall what she sees in him.

Hitchcock, by not oversimplifying this situation, has challenged his viewers to recognize that a single individual can be both self-deceptively foolish and, in 'Minta's words, "a strong, sensible man." Only at the film's end are these two facets integrated, when Sweetland, depressed at being rejected once more, admits his failure to the faithful housekeeper. "I've got a lot of faults," he says, "but there's good in me yet, 'Minta." Gazing at his late wife's empty chair, he imagines (in double exposure) each woman sitting there and rejecting his proposal. Then, in the same shot, the real 'Minta sits down and Sweetland realizes that she belongs there. Shedding his illusions about himself, he tells her, "I'm offering myself so humble as a worm, but I'd like to mention one thing in my favor—a little child can lead me." The truth about Sweetland, which he finally understands, is the fact that he needs someone to take care of him.

The Farmer's Wife transcends its origin in bucolic comedy to become an examination of marriage. Araminta's belief that there is "something magical in the married state" is countered by the farm's handyman, who declares, "Holy Matrimony be a proper steam roller for flattening the hope out of a man and the joy out of a woman." While the couples in *Easy Virtue*, *The Ring*, and *The Manxman* would probably agree with the handyman, *The Farmer's Wife* demonstrates, if not the achievement of "something magical," then at least the possibility of its achievement. That possibility, though, does not involve romantic fantasies. Instead, it requires that a woman see past the self-deceptions and incompetence of her man, accepting them as part of the person and responding to the vulnerability and helplessness that he hides, mostly from himself.

Murder!, 1930

CHAPTER FOUR
SOUND AND IMAGE

"If I have to shoot a long scene con-
tinuously I always feel
I am losing grip on it, from a
cinematic point of view."
— Alfred Hitchcock[1]

"Dialogue should simply be a sound
among other sounds."
— Alfred Hitchcock to
François Truffaut, 1962

Seen today, Hitchcock's silent films hold up as solid and satisfying, if sometimes inconsistent, works. All seem made with
seriousness and commitment (despite what Hitchcock might imply
40 years later) and all use their medium with intelligence and, at
times, insight. Having thus defined and developed his art in the context of silent films, with their emphasis on visual communication,
Hitchcock naturally considered that medium to be the "the purest
form of cinema." Although silent films lacked voices and noises,
he told François Truffaut in 1962:

> ...there was no need to go to the other
> extreme and completely abandon the
> technique of the pure motion picture,
> the way they did when sound came
> in.... In many of the films now being
> made, there is very little cinema: they

In *Blackmail***, Anny Ondra played Alice White, but because of her accent another actress spoke the character's lines.**

are mostly what I call "photographs of
people talking."

The transition to sound in Britain began in 1929 and lasted into
1931. During that time, the new technology's limitations made the
rules. Specifically, it was not possible to cut and splice the sound
track, so in order to maintain synchronization of sound and image
all of a scene's shots had to be filmed simultaneously with separate
cameras. Inevitably, this limited the number and variety of shots a
director could use in a scene, and it hindered his ability to compose
and light those shots. Also, microphones picked up noise made
by the cameras, so until quieter equipment could be developed

The restlessness and complacency of Alice White lead to an event that abruptly changes her life in *Blackmail*.

the cameras and their operators were placed in large, soundproof booths, which severely reduced the ability to create moving camera shots.

By the end of 1931, equipment had evolved so that these limitations were overcome and directors could again take charge. But thoughtful directors like Hitchcock still had to decide how best to use the new medium. A sound film, after all, was not just a silent film with sound added, nor was it a recorded play. A new aesthetic had to be discovered, one which integrated sound and image in mutually dependent ways, with both needed for full comprehension

Actor John Longden and Ex-Detective Sergeant Bishop play Scotland Yard detectives about to make an arrest at the beginning of *Blackmail*.

of a scene. Starting with his first sound films, Hitchcock faced this challenge and sought to express his characters' thoughts and feelings through the new medium.

Hitchcock initially shot *Blackmail* (1929) as a silent feature. To do so, he reconceived its source, a play, by replacing words with images that hold a viewer's attention and communicate information. Later, he re-filmed some scenes with synchronized dialogue, while adding music and sound effects to the rest. As a result, the sound version of Blackmail is far more visual than most early talkies, and critics praised Hitchcock's dramatic use of sound and picture. However, except for a few key scenes, *Blackmail* is not truly a sound film, but a silent film containing sound segments.

Instead of continuing in the direction suggested by *Blackmail*—i.e., imposing the silent film aesthetic on the sound film

In the opening of *Juno and the Paycock* (1929), a speech by the Orator (Barry Fitzgerald) is interrupted by machine gun fire. (Photofest)

medium—Hitchcock next adapted three more plays and treated their use of dialogue with greater "respect." First, he filmed Sean O'Casey's Irish classic, *Juno and the Paycock* (1929), which added to his prestige as a "serious" director. Then, the whodunit, *Murder!* (1930), allowed him to relax a bit with his material. He followed this with the serious social observations of John Galsworthy's *The Skin Game* (1931).

The O'Casey and Galsworthy films have somewhat unfairly been dismissed by later critics, and at times by Hitchcock himself, as atypical exercises inconsistent with the director's interests and sensibility. This view seems derived from two facts: Hitchcock did not substantially revise these plays, and they are not thrillers or crime stories. At the time, however, *Juno* and *The Skin Game* were quite consistent with Hitchcock's position as a major director of main-

Alice (Anny Ondra) drifts into danger in *Blackmail*.

stream subjects; in fact, before *Blackmail*, he had made only one thriller, so films in that genre were the exception, not the rule.

Not only was Hitchcock not committed to filming crime stories at this point in his career, but *Blackmail* and *Murder!* reveal his self-conscious amusement at the form. *Blackmail* includes a joke at Hitchcock's own expense when a policeman says that he wants to see the movie, Fingerprints, because its makers are "bound to get all the details wrong." His girlfriend responds that she heard "they've got a real criminal to direct it, so as to be on the safe side." Similarly, *Murder!*'s main character once acted in Pistols for Two, which he says is the kind of play "the critics describe as 'a highbrow shocker.'" Is that also what Hitchcock hoped to convince his critics they were watching?

Certainly, Blackmail does connect with *The Lodger* in important ways. Like Daisy in that film, Alice White (Anny Ondra, with Joan

Barry's voice) is an average, working class woman whose boyfriend, Frank (John Longden), is a police detective, and both heroines drift from secure positions into an unpredictable, potentially dangerous relationship with another man. Alice's mental state, however, has less in common with Daisy than with characters in Hitchcock's non-thrillers. Like the heroine of *Champagne*, Alice quarrels with her boyfriend and decides to have a good time without him. Bored and petulant, she is irritated that Frank's job makes him late for their evening date. Already planning to meet a man she hardly knows, Alice bickers with Frank, saying that she doesn't want to go to a movie because "I've seen everything worth seeing," a line which also suggests her sense of being trapped in a mundane life. (Iris, in 1938's *The Lady Vanishes*, reveals a similarly smug assumption when she says, "I've been everywhere and done everything.")

Alice, like many of Hitchcock's male characters, is self-deceptive and over-confident. Moving out of her depth, she flirts with a force she thinks she can control by tempting the more sophisticated other man, an artist (Cyril Ritchard). After being invited to his apartment, she asserts that it would "take more than a man to frighten me." She enters, but her flirtation backfires when the artist attacks her. Desperately she grasps a nearby knife and stabs him to death. In *Champagne*, a man's attack had turned out to be a figment of the heroine's imagination, but in *Blackmail* Alice's restlessness and complacency lead to a real event which abruptly changes her life.

It is wrong to consider Blackmail more "personal" to Hitchcock just because it deals with a crime and its investigation. This premise is not significant in itself. Instead, like the premise of any other kind of story, it leads to an examination of the resulting emotions and conflicts, such as Alice's guilt and Frank's dilemma when he discovers her involvement in the case.

At this stage in his career, Hitchcock was a highly regarded director whose talent transcended genre. At the same time, he was not just a director-for-hire. Even *Juno and the Paycock* and *The Skin Game* are not slavish filmings of other people's creations; instead, they are

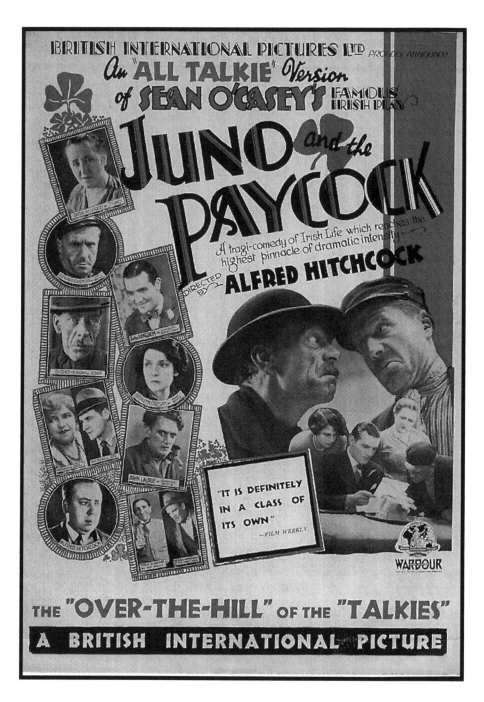

proudly credited as "Adapted and Directed by Alfred Hitchcock," with Alma Reville also listed as author of the scenarios.

Although Hitchcock's version of *Juno* was unusually faithful to its source, that was due less to O'Casey's status than to the fact that it was one of Hitchcock's favorite plays. (Bogdanovich, 15) Specifically, he "liked the story, the mood, the characters, and the blend of humor and tragedy very much." (Truffaut, 48) *Juno*'s characters and situations are, in fact, reminiscent of some he had previously depicted. Like Hitchcock's other male characters, Captain Jack Boyle (Edward Chapman), the "paycock" (peacock) of the title, is both over-confident of his abilities and unreliable, avoiding work by claiming to have pains in his legs and lying about having been a ship's captain. Meanwhile, his faithful, determined wife, Juno (Sara Allgood), supports him and the family, financially and emotionally.

Another link with Hitchcock's prior films is the guilt endured by the son, Johnny (John Laurie), who has informed on another man and caused his death. This situation evokes Alice's, in *Blackmail*, except that the viewer is aware of Alice's burden throughout, but only gradually learns about Johnny's. Also, Boyle's daughter, like Alice, is lured away from a reliable but common man by someone more sophisticated but less trustworthy; her parallel to Kate, in *The Manxman*, is even closer, because in both cases the second man is a lawyer and the woman becomes pregnant by him.

Hitchcock probably also responded to the way *Juno* depicts daily life carrying on amid sudden death during the Irish "troubles." More specifically, at one point in O'Casey's play a character reports the discovery of her son's corpse, which was "lyin' for a whole night stretched out on the side of a lonely counthry lane, with his head, his darlin' head, that I often kissed an' fondled, half hidden in the wather of a runnin' brook." Hitchcock's film condenses this statement to what (in the character's thick accent) sounds like "found out in a lonely country lane, pierced with bullets, lying down by the side of a gargling brook." This version places greater emphasis on the incongruous setting and is, surely, the origin of Hitchcock's

Neighbors react to the crime that begins the plot of *Murder!*

famous comment that "murder by a babbling brook" interests him more than "murder in a dark and noisome alley."[2]

Murder! involves an innocent person accused of a killing, a subject to which Hitchcock would return many times, but rather than detailing that character's suspenseful predicament, it follows an amateur detective's pursuit of clues. As a result, it connects less with *The Lodger* and *Blackmail* than with aspects of Hitchcock's other films. In *Easy Virtue*, for example, a jury bases its judgment on surface appearances, and in *Murder!* the jurors assume that the defendant (Nora Baring) is guilty mainly because she doesn't deny committing the crime. *Murder!* also includes considerable comedy, usually involving such subsidiary characters as an unemployed stage manager and his wife, whose lower middle-class existence is depicted in an extended scene as their child practices the piano while their landlady demands the rent.

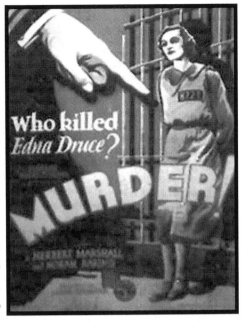

On another occasion, the detective, Sir John Menier (Herbert Marshall), has spent the night in the guest room of a policeman's house and is still in bed when the landlady (Una O'Connor) enters, carrying a crying baby. Soon, other children swarm around the uncomfortable Sir John, with one even crawling onto the bed. The mother's threat to an unruly child—"I'll have your father take you to the police station"—recalls Hitchcock's often-repeated story about his father sending him to the local station with a note asking the officer to lock him in a cell. *Murder!*'s depiction of intrusive children may be related to the fact that, on July 7, 1928, Hitchcock himself became a father. In this context, one should recall the director's cameo appearance in *Blackmail*, as a placid subway passenger disturbed by an impish child.

The most interesting aspect of *Murder!* is not the mystery but a motif inspired by the plot's theatrical setting: The victim, the defendant, and the killer are all actors and Sir John is both an actor and a playwright, a man who now sets out to revise a script that life has written. As Sir John explains, "Artists have a double function. We use life to create art and we use art to—how shall I put it?—to criticize life." His desire to "fulfill our double function" also appears to be Hitchcock's aim. In the process, Hitchcock explores the distinction between living and performing, between doing and acting.

In a lengthy scene of the police questioning actors backstage during a performance, the players shift back and forth between their

Hitchcock cleverly juxtaposes the theatre scene and a prison scene in *Murder!*

characters and their supposedly true selves, as Hitchcock playfully contrasts the farce enacted on stage with this serious aspect of "reality." Later, Shakespeare's *Hamlet* inspires Sir John to trap his suspect (Esme Percy) by having him audition for a play about the murder. In this way, he hopes to expose an actor who is, in real life, pretending to be an innocent man reading the part of a murderer, a "role" he has in fact already played in reality. When the man realizes he is trapped, he gives one last public "performance" by hanging himself during his circus trapeze act, in which he wears a woman's costume. (This scene may have been inspired by Fritz Lang's 1928 German film, *Spione* [Spies], in which a trapped criminal kills himself during his stage performance while wearing a clown's costume.)

The theater motif also influences Hitchcock's visual choices, as when he cuts from a curtain rising in front of a stage setting to the window in a cell door rising to reveal the convicted woman within. Then, on a close-up of the prisoner's face, we hear the play being performed, only without her in her usual role. This juxtaposition of sound and image establishes both what is happening elsewhere and what she is thinking about; it also suggests that the woman now plays a new role, this time in a real-life drama.

Much later, she has been freed and the final scene opens in a living room, where Sir John waits. The woman whose life he has saved enters and he kisses her hand. The camera then pulls back (as it had in *Downhill*) to reveal that the scene is being enacted on stage, in a play probably written by Sir John, who recently rewrote the plot of the woman's "real" life. This on-stage encounter between the two people could easily—but not inevitably—reflect the couple's off-stage relationship. The theater's curtain then falls, ending both the play and the film.

In *Murder!*, Hitchcock blurs the distinction between reality and melodrama, but *The Skin Game* directly confronts a real social issue, the challenge modern industry poses to the landed gentry's traditional outlook, as represented by two antagonistic families, the Hornblowers and the Hillcrists. The success of his factories leads Mr. Hornblower (Edmund Gwenn) to buy more land so he can put up more "chimneys," which requires evicting elderly tenants from their homes and cutting down trees. This destruction of nature and humanity in the name of a dubious "progress" is the opposite of what the Hillcrists represent.

In this situation, Hornblower seems cast as the villain and the Hillcrists as heroic preservationists. However, author John Galsworthy does not oversimplify matters and refuses to ascribe "right" or "wrong" to either side, a subtlety that no doubt attracted Hitchcock. The Hillcrists do advocate an appealing way of life and they do appreciate the human worth of poor tenants, but they also reject Hornblower "as a neighbor" because he lacks breeding. Mr. Hillcrist (C.V. France) will not shake hands with Hornblower, and Mrs. Hillcrist (Helen Haye) refuses to visit his daughter-in-law, Chloe. Although Hornblower offers to change his plans if the Hillcrists will only treat him and his family with respect, they refuse.

Matters do not rest here. Soon, Mrs. Hillcrist—without consulting her husband—uses blackmail to defend her higher principles.

With her past exposed, the distraught Chloe Hornblower (Phyllis Konstam) throws herself into the swimming pool in *The Skin Game* (1931).

Suspecting that Chloe is not what she seems, Mrs. Hillcrist discovers that she once worked as a professional co-respondant (the woman whom the law required a husband be found with before he could be granted a divorce). Told by his wife that she plans to threaten Hornblower with this information, Hillcrist gains a viewer's respect by declaring, "It's repugnant! I won't do it!" Mrs. Hillcrist, sounding eerily like Mrs. Whittaker in Easy Virtue and Philip's mother-surrogate in The Manxman, righteously asks, "If you had a son tricked into marrying such a woman, would you wish to remain ignorant of it?"

After Mrs. Hillcrist ignores her husband and tells Hornblower about Chloe's past, Mr. Hillcrist reveals sympathy for Chloe when he tells his daughter, "I should be the last to judge." Meanwhile, Chloe's husband learns the truth and, childishly petulant, rejects his wife. And so we have four figures already encountered in

There is much that is visual in *Blackmail*.

Hitchcock's films: a weak but fairly dignified father; a strong and arrogant mother; a self-centered, unreliable husband; and a misjudged, rejected wife. In terms of content, then, Hitchcock's first sound films have much in common with his silents and contribute to a consistent creative evolution.

Another charge often leveled against these films (except Blackmail) is that they are visually static, but the situation is not that simple. Hitchcock realized that a complete reworking of his material was easier in the silent film era. It was one thing to communicate visually *instead of* aurally; it is quite another to integrate dialogue and sounds with images so that both aspects contribute to the viewer's understanding of a scene.

In his 1929-31 films, Hitchcock can be seen striving for that combination, while still facing the new medium's technical limitations. At times, he includes a totally visual sequence that rivals any in his silent films. Elsewhere, he blends image with sound in

The painting of a jester silently accuses Alice in Hitchcock's first sound film, *Blackmail.*

imaginative and meaningful ways. Even in his more static scenes, Hitchcock often manages to include some elements of visual communication.

Blackmail contains much that is totally visual. The opening, for example, is a nine-minute sequence that depicts a criminal's arrest, from his capture through his being questioned and jailed, all without synchronized dialogue. Also, on four occasions, Hitchcock uses a painting of a laughing, pointing jester and gives it different overtones in each context. When it first appears, in the artist's apartment, Alice merely giggles at it. Soon after, having stabbed the artist, she abruptly confronts the jester, whose laugh and pointing finger now serve as a grim accusation. Later, Hitchcock dissolves from a man who is blackmailing Alice to a shot of the jester, which unobtrusively depicts the man as a mocking conscience. Ultimately, the blackmailer falls to his death during a chase and Scotland Yard assumes he is the murderer, so Alice and Frank are free to spend their lives together, but a final view of the painting reminds them of their secret and of the inner burden she will always bear.

Juno and the Paycock lacks such purely visual moments, but *Murder!* contains a brief, but intriguing, break with visual reality. To convey a visitor's perception of Sir John's intimidating office, Hitchcock shows the man's feet sinking into the thick, spongy carpet (it looks as though he is walking on a waterbed). In a more familiar vein, a shot of Sir John's hands leafing through his appointment book reveals that he will meet his suspect at 1:30 on Monday; Tuesday's page is blank, but on Wednesday's is written the name of the convicted murderess, followed by a question mark, which carries life-or-death implications for her. Sir John then flips back to Monday and his wristwatch shows that the time is slightly after 1:30. During this shot, the viewer realizes the deadline Sir John faces and the importance of the coming interview.

Although the conflict in *The Skin Game* is established through dialogue, Hitchcock does transform a minor incident into a visual embodiment of the film's situation. When a flock of sheep on the village road blocks the movement of a truck, the director intercuts close shots of the angry driver, the sheep, the herder, a sign that reads "Hornblower Potteries," and the driver's hand blowing his horn. This last image is not just a pun on Hornblower's name, for it conveys both his determination to carry industrial progress forward and his frustration at being inhibited by the area's bucolic ways.

Still, for every scene that uses images expressively, these films include several long, visually static conversations, but even these scenes possess visual elements that contribute to the final effect. Typical is a nearly four-minute scene in Blackmail composed almost entirely of one shot of Alice and Frank seated at a restaurant table. Eventually, Frank leaves to fetch Alice's glove from where she left it and Hitchcock finally starts to edit: He cuts to a close-up of Alice,

Captain Boyle (Edward Chapman) and "Joxer" Daly (Sidney Morgan) enjoy a drink and song with Juno (Sara Allgood) and Mrs. Madigan (Marie O'Neil) in *Juno and the Paycock.*

to a note she removes from her bag, and then to shots of the artist arriving and of her signaling to him. This editing may be minimal, but through it Hitchcock conveys important information visually.

Because Hitchcock admired the play *Juno and the Paycock*, his film version is content to communicate thoughts and emotions through the characters' voices. Occasionally, though, Hitchcock shows Johnny while we hear others conversing off-screen; this implies a relationship between that character and what is being said, and it prepares viewers for the revelation that Johnny is the informer being discussed. Hitchcock uses a similar sound-image juxtaposition in *The Skin Game*, holding on a shot of Hornblower as Mrs. Hillcrist's voice describes Chloe's tainted past.

In *Murder!*, too, the characters' thoughts are usually verbalized, not visualized; as a result, many scenes are slowly paced and

In *The Skin Game*, Hornblower (Edmund Gwenn) and his son (John Lundgen) do not realize that Chloe has just recognized a man from her past.

dialogue-laden. In one case, two women talk while preparing tea and then walk back and forth between two rooms, with the camera following their every step. *The Skin Game* also contains such single-shot conversations, with Hitchcock's camera sometimes moving from speaker to speaker, awkwardly crossing empty space instead of efficiently cutting among the characters. Elsewhere, though, Hitchcock relates the photography to the action in useful ways. When Hornblower first visits the Hillcrists, the camera spends more than four minutes moving with him through the room, so that other people are seen only if he is near them. This gives the shot visual variety, while linking the viewer with the dynamic Hornblower. However, everything important is still established and developed through dialogue.

Hitchcock must have been thinking of such scenes when he wrote, in 1937:

> I am willing to work with the long un-
> interrupted shot.... But if I have to shoot
> a long scene continuously I always feel
> I am losing grip on it, from a cinematic
> point of view. The camera, I feel, is
> simply standing there, *hoping* to catch
> something with a visual point to it.

He preferred

> ...to put my film together on the screen,
> not simply to photograph something
> that has been put together already in the
> form of a long piece of stage acting.[3]

At least, Hitchcock's conversation scenes are not as tedious as some other directors', thanks to his use of some visual qualities and to his material's inherent interest. (It is worth noting that, in the late 1940s, Hitchcock discarded his familiar procedure and used long takes in *Rope* [1948] and *Under Capricorn* [1949], after which he returned to editing as his main stylistic device.)

In each of his early sound films (except *Juno*), Hitchcock also employs subjectivity, as he had in his silent films. *Blackmail* presents Alice White's mental state in a strikingly

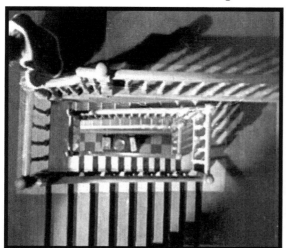

Hitchcock films the staircase from above as Alice leaves the apartment in *Blackmail*.

vis-ual sequence after she leaves the artist's apartment. As she walks home, the camera moves alongside her, and the people who pass by in the foreground and background are double exposed, which turns them into ghostly figures that barely register on her attention. Then, a traffic policeman's extended forearm reminds her of the dead man's arm, a theater marquee ironically announces "A New Comedy," and in an advertising sign, a hand shaking a cocktail turns into one holding a knife.

A less extended example occurs in *Murder!* while the killer performs his trapeze act. As he swings, we see shots from his perspective, over which Hitchcock superimposes the faces of people whose lives he has affected, images that evoke both guilt and a loss of equilibrium, and that motivate his suicide. The same technique appears in *The Skin Game*, when Chloe sees a man from her past talking with a Hillcrist employee. Hitchcock conveys her reaction in a shot of the two talking, over which is superimposed the face of the man she recognizes, which repeatedly zooms into tight close-up. Also in *The Skin Game*, Hillcrist's view of a pastoral setting dissolves into a factory, revealing his "vision" of nature and tradition replaced by industry and progress.

On many occasions, Hitchcock goes beyond the purely visual by making creative use of his new medium's possibilities. Sometimes, his editing illustrates, or comments on, what is being said. In *Blackmail*, as Alice stands outside the artist's door, she mentions that she lives around the corner and Hitchcock matches her description of the building with a shot of it. When Sir John, in *Murder!*, stands outside the house where he will spend the night, he asks, "You don't think that I'd better sleep at the Red Lion after all, do you?" At the mention of the inn, Hitchcock cuts to a table set with a large meal and a bottle of wine, a very welcoming image of what Sir John would prefer.

In a more elaborate blend of sound and image, *Murder!* summarizes the attempt to locate the missing suspect, with dialogue moving the plot forward while the images keep track of the woman whose life hangs in the balance. On the soundtrack, we hear voices

Alice reacts to the butter knife at the breakfast table the morning after the murder in *Blackmai*l.

asking about the suspect, but we see a weather vane as its arrow moves in various directions, never settling on one. This is intercut with shots of the prisoner in her cell and of a shadow that moves up a wall as the sun changes position and the day progresses, a shadow that gradually reveals the shape of the gallows that awaits her. This imaginative sequence ends as the voices locate the man over a close-up of the noose's shadow.

In his silent films, Hitchcock often used distorted images to reflect a character's subjective state, and in *Blackmail* he does the same with sound. When Alice joins her family at breakfast, a neighbor enters to gossip about the previous night's murder and as Hitchcock shows a close-up of Alice's face, the visitor's voice becomes a muffled rumble, except for the word "knife," which stands out clearly in Alice's mind and the viewer's ears. Thus, a noncommittal image gains meaning by its juxtaposition with subjectively distorted sound.

This may have felt like too complete a break with reality, for in *Murder!* Hitchcock again uses subjective sound, but this time without any distortion. Sir John is the last jury member to resist a guilty verdict, so the others try to convince him of their position. At first, the scene's dialogue is realistic, but as the jurors confront Sir John with various arguments, they repeat, "Any answer to that, Sir John?" in a kind of choral chant. After this happens several times, Hitchcock tracks in on Sir John's face while the voices continue their questions, which places us in his mental state by presenting the flood of words that overwhelms him.

Although this does not distort reality the way *Blackmail*'s knife scene had, the choral effect does stylize it somewhat. However, in another scene from *Murder!* Hitchcock achieves aural subjectivity without modifying reality at all. While shaving in his bathroom, Sir John considers the case and, over a shot of his face, the man's off-screen, inner voice articulates his thoughts.

Nothing in *The Skin Game* is quite as internalized as these scenes, but Hitchcock still juxtaposes sound and image in a subjective way. During an auction, one shot (lasting nearly a minute and a half) is taken from the auctioneer's point of view, moving rapidly from face to face as he locates each bidder. Shortly before, when an official read the conditions of the sale, the sound of his voice was cut off, although coughing and other noises could still be heard. This is among Hitchcock's more idiosyncratic touches, because it represents what might be called "generalized subjectivity"—the director doesn't establish it as any one person's perception, but instead implies that everyone has tuned out this required recital.

During 1931, the limitations of early sound equipment were overcome and Hitchcock, as if anxious to make the most of the opportunity, began to develop his own project, one not adapted from a play. These plans, though, were interrupted when the studio maneuvered him into co-writing and directing a film of the mystery play, *Number Seventeen* (1932).

"I've never gone in for the creaking-door type of suspense," Hitchcock asserted in 1957,[4] but in *Number Seventeen* the director who preferred murder by a babbling brook to death in a dark alley

In *Number Seventeen* (1932), the bareheaded Ben (Leon M. Lion) is as confused about these men's identities as the film's viewers are. (Photofest)

indulges in an elaborate assortment of creaking-door clichés. More than half the film is spent in a dark, deserted house, where events occur seemingly without reason. "You don't have to do nothin' in

Hero and heroine (Anne Grey and John Stuart) have temporarily lost control of the situations in *Number Seventeen*. (Photofest)

this 'ere 'ouse," declares an old tramp (Leon M. Lion) who blunders into the plot. "Just stand still and things 'appen. Everything's loopy 'ere." Assorted characters arrive at midnight with odd justifications,

Ben encounters another mysterious stranger in n *Number Seventeen.* **(Photofest)**

a corpse appears and abruptly vanishes, a mute woman suddenly speaks, and identities prove as nebulous as the shadows that glide along walls and reach toward doorknobs. Then, after exhausting his supply of inexplicable events, Hitchcock sorts out the heroes from the villains and sends them on a wild, 10-minute chase as a commandeered bus pursues a train, which crashes into a ferry just leaving its dock.

Although his mind may have been elsewhere, Hitchcock probably enjoyed making this entertaining trifle. If nothing else, it allowed him for the first time to feature one of his abiding passions, railroad trains. Then, upon completing *Number Seventeen,* Hitchcock returned to *Rich and Strange*, his most personal project since *The Ring.* He surely expected that it would further strengthen his position as Britain's most prominent filmmaker. Instead, Rich and Strange became Hitchcock's last film for B.I.P. and sent him into a professional and creative crisis.

CHAPTER FIVE
RICH AND STRANGE

"I have to know where I am going
every second of the time."
— Alfred Hitchcock[1]

In 1937, Alfred Hitchcock wrote that if he could direct any kind of film without concern for box office appeal he would make "travel films with a personal element in them: that would be a new field."[2]   Actually, it would not have been entirely new, because he had already directed such a film, *Rich and Strange*. Although it failed at the box office in 1931-32, Hitchcock retained a fondness for the picture, and rightly so. *Rich and Strange* may not be his most accessible film, but it is intelligent, heartfelt, and uncompromising in often surprising ways. While too rich in content and form to be immediately digestible, and too strange in its implications and style to be a comfortable comedy or drama, this film is continually rewarding in its challenges and insights.

One reason for this is the fact that Hitchcock put into practice a theory, stated in *Murder!*, about the double function of artists:

We use life to create art, and we use
art to...criticize life.

In *Rich and Strange*, Hitchcock mixed his art and his life in an honest and extensive fashion. The film is, in fact, as close to a psychological self-analysis as any he ever made. At the same time, *Rich and Strange* communicates a sense of freedom and enthusiasm, a youthful delight in creation, as if its maker were

A production still of Fred's walk home from work in *Rich and Strange* (1932).

rediscovering the possibilities of film. This is especially true of the early scenes, many of which are satiric, broadly stylized, and highly visual. After this somewhat bitter whimsy, the film becomes quietly dramatic, then shifts into stark seriousness.

Rich and Strange begins with Fred Hill (Henry Kendall) at his job, working with numbers at one of the many desks in a large, regimented office. As a clock marks the workday's end, everyone rises and marches out in almost perfect unison. For Fred, we soon realize, his job is frustrating and his life a series of petty annoyances. His umbrella refuses to open, at least until he arrives home and he doesn't need it any more. On the subway he has trouble getting his newspaper unfolded, the crowds jostle him, and a sign invites him to "Dine at the Majestic" as he stands near a man eating a sloppy sandwich. By now, an ad in the paper seems intended for him: "Are you satisfied with your present circumstances?" it asks. The subway scene ends as Fred loses his balance, a subtle summation of his mental state.

This four-minute opening contains no dialogue, creating its effects by purely visual means, including careful control of the actors' movements, an elaborate tracking shot in the office, and precise editing between Fred and the things he notices. The result is much more ambitious than the equally visual opening of *Blackmail*, which seeks only to depict events. Here, Hitchcock creates a complex, ambivalent tone. On the one hand, Fred's office world is mocked as repetitive, mundane, and stifling, an atmosphere Hitchcock surely recalled from his own first job, as a clerk at the Henley Telegraph and Cable Company. As a result, a viewer feels encouraged to identify with Fred's dissatisfaction, but the situation has another side to it.

Although Fred is out of step with those around him, Hitchcock does not present that as a positive characteristic. The other employees leave the office in secure, confident pairs and open their umbrellas with crisp, efficient motions. Fred, however, is alone and awkward; only he fails to control his umbrella. If Fred differs from the others, it is not because he is better than they are. Rather, he is incapable of functioning effectively in this environment, and later it comes as no surprise that he is equally dysfunctional in the larger, outside world. Only in the confines of his home can Fred be what he thinks he is, and that is because Emily (Joan Barry), his deferential wife of eight years, supports his illusions.

As Fred enters his standardized row house, the musical score mocks him with the tune, "There's No Place Like Home." Even there, he is haunted by echoes of his tedious job, with the radio about to broadcast a lecture on accountancy. "I want some life!" Fred announces in desperate tones. "Life, I tell you! Like that—" he adds, indicating the picture of a ship that hangs on a wall. "The best place for us," he concludes, like a spoiled child, "is the gas ovens." The contented Em is disturbed by such talk, because "we've a roof over our heads, food, beds, oh and lots of things."

At this point, Hitchcock dispenses with narrative realism and has Fred receive a letter from an uncle, who conveniently offers the money Fred needs to change his life. (This initiating event derives from *Downhill*, in which Roddy is left £30,000 by his godmother, and *Juno and the Paycock*, in which Boyle learns of a substantial

The Hills at home: Fred (Henry Kendall) is bored, but Emily (Joan Barry) is satisfied.

inheritance.) As Em reads this letter, in a subjective shot the words "money to experience all the life you want by travelling" move across the screen in an extreme close-up, giving the news a visual force that matches its emotional impact.

The Hills' journey begins with a title that quotes from Shakespeare's *The Tempest*: "Doth suffer a sea change/Into something rich and strange." This is an ambiguous, even cryptic, citation because, although it speaks of change, it does so in reference to a drowned person's decomposing corpse. Its context is death, not the simple enjoyment of life that Fred expects. Also, this printed intertitle is the first of several that Hitchcock uses in *Rich and Strange*, but these titles are not like those in silent films, which generally contained dialogue or factual statements. Instead, they serve as the voice of the author-director, who comments on his own story and makes unusually direct contact with his audience.

The next three titles identify the challenges that even a Paris visit presents to the Hills, with each one involving disorientation or a loss of stability. "To get to Paris you have to cross the Channel," we are told. After boarding the ship, the over-confident Fred declares, "I ought to have gone in for the sea," but when he tries to take Em's picture, his view of her through the lens is unsteady and he becomes seasick, while the more stable Em is unaffected  (anticipating what the film later reveals about their relationship). In a good example of Hitchcock's economical mixture of dialogue and picture, Fred tries to hide his illness from Em by saying he will get some magazines for her. As he leaves, Em looks down at the magazines she already holds and says, "No, but—," which ends the scene. She need not say more, for we understand everything from the objects the director has shown.

Then, "To get to the Folies Bergère you have to cross Paris." Hitchcock evokes the Hills' fragmented impressions of the city by jump-cutting from a close-up of them looking in one direction to an identical shot of them looking in the other direction, with the turning of their heads omitted. This pair of shots is then alternated with views of Parisian landmarks: the Arch of Triumph, the Eiffel Tower, Notre Dame Cathedral, and a public urinal! Hitchcock also illustrates the overwhelmed couple's impression of the hectic city by speeding up the traffic's movement. At the Folies Bergère, the naïve Em looks at the bare-breasted chorus girls and says, "The curtain's gone up too soon—they're not dressed!"

"And to get to your room you have to cross the hotel lounge." Fred and Em have stopped at a bar and now, inebriated, they have trouble walking through the hotel's lobby. Disoriented, Fred mistakes the elevator's circular floor indicator for a clock and re-sets his watch by it. Other comic moments reflect, with a touch of sadness, the couple's relationship and their perceptions. When

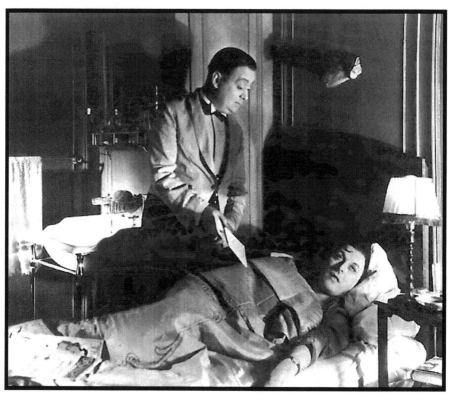

The seasick Fred reacts when a steward brings him the menu. (Photofest)

Fred presents Em with a silky nightgown, she responds, "I couldn't wear this. People will think we aren't married!"

In Marseilles, the Hills board a cruise ship to start the main part of their journey, a tour across the Mediterranean and through the Suez Canal to Colombo and Singapore. Again, Fred immediately becomes seasick and (like the heroine's boyfriend in *Champagne*) spends part of the cruise in bed. When a steward brings him a menu, the words—"lobster mayonnaise," "cream sherry trifle," "gorgonzola cheese"—literally leap off the page and aggravate his distress. Like "Captain" Boyle in *Juno and the Paycock*, Fred only imagines himself a sailor, but this time seasickness reveals not only the man's self-deception but also his inability to maintain a psychological balance. Em's reaction to Fred's weakness reveals her character: With blind confidence, she defends her husband, unaware of the contradiction in her statement that he's "really a very good sailor, but he's not used to it."

Fred's journey becomes the most explicit version yet of what Hitchcock's characters often endure: an excursion from a secure, domestic environment to self-exposure and humiliation. Such journeys are inevitably linked with disorientation and instability, with a loss of balance and perspective, as the character comes to realize that he (or, occasionally, she) is an outsider, an exile, someone out of step with others. For example, Roddy, in *Downhill*, leaves home for the Continent and completely loses his grip in Marseilles, the city where Fred Hill's excursion begins. John Whittaker is also out of his depth in the south of France, where he meets and marries Larita Filton. Samuel

Roddy (Ivor Novello) loses his grip and faces ruin after leaving home in *Downhill.*

Sweetland, however, only has to leave his farm to be humbled, and Alice White loses control of her life around the corner from her parents' house. For *Champagne*, Hitchcock had devised a similar plot (not used) about an innocent girl who works nailing down the lids of champagne crates. Watching as the bottles are shipped to Paris, she wonders about the appealing, romantic lives led there. "And then she eventually gravitated to the city," recalled Hitchcock, "and became a kind of whore and was put through the mill." At the story's end, she would return to her town and her job, disillusioned.[3]

In his fondness for German silent films, Hitchcock may have encountered a work by writer-director Karl Grune, *Die Strasse* (*The Street*; 1923), in which a stable citizen leaves the security of his middle class home and is taken advantage of and physically attacked. This type of situation would certainly have struck a chord in Hitchcock. Like his own characters, the insecure director was "never satisfied" and "ill at ease" with what he called "the ordinary"[4] but, unlike them, he resisted plunging into the unknown. By sending fictional characters forth in his place, he dramatized what might happen and thereby justified his own wariness.

In this way, Hitchcock's films—especially *Rich and Strange*—reflect their director's personality, which was both attracted to and afraid of the unfamiliar. In Hitchcock's youth, the idea of travel fascinated him, yet he never ventured beyond London.

> When I was a child, to satisfy my passion for boats, I had an immense map in my room on which I indicated, with the help of little flags, the exact place of the navigating buildings on the seas and the oceans of the world. It was enough for me to look at it to believe myself captain on a long cruise![5]

Hitchcock also became

> ...completely familiar with the map of New York. I used to send away for train schedules—that was my hobby—and I knew many of the timetables by heart. Years before I ever came here, I could describe New York, tell you where the theatres and stores were located.

He admitted that he had

> ...often wondered about the fact that I made no attempt to visit America until 1937; I'm still puzzled about that.[6]

Although intrigued by the idea of travel, Hitchcock resisted the actual experience, and as a young man he was also unacquainted with other aspects of life. At the age of 23, he confessed:

I'd never been out with a girl in my life. I'd never had a drink in my life.[7]

Even when he went to Germany to make films, he felt comfortable only in the familiar atmosphere of a studio. Elsewhere, he was a curious, nervous observer, not a confident participant. In Berlin in 1924, he and his more worldly associates "wound up in a night club where men danced with each other. There were also female couples." (Hitchcock drew on this memory in *Champagne*, when the heroine grows uncomfortable in the nightclub where she works because she notices two women dancing together.)

Alma and Hitch on location in the early 1920s.

Later that evening, Hitchcock continued:

> ...two German girls, one around 19 and the other about 30 years old, volunteered to drive us home. The car stopped in front of a hotel and they insisted that we go in. In the hotel room they made several propositions, to which I stolidly replied, "*Nein, nein.*" Then we had several cognacs, and finally the two German girls got into bed. And the young girl in our party, who was a student, put on her glasses to make sure she wouldn't miss anything.[8]

This reference to the student's glasses suggests an inspiration for the various characters in Hitchcock's films who use glasses, binoculars, and monocles to help them see better.

Other influences on *Rich and Strange* relate to Hitchcock's life with Alma. He proposed to her as they crossed the English Channel on a ship that, he recalled in 1956:

> ...was floundering in a most desperate way and so was Alma, who was seasick.[9]

Later, at the start of their honeymoon, they had lunch in Paris with actress Nita Naldi and, according to John Russell Taylor, they drank so much that (like Fred and Em) they "reeled back to their hotel... with the carpet in the lobby lurching and heaving beneath them."[10]

Several years after, Hitchcock and Alma (and their daughter, Patricia) took a winter cruise along the coast of Africa and to the Caribbean, which may have inspired the journey in *Rich and Strange*. Then, when he and Alma began developing that film's script, they visited Paris to do research. Although they thought they were attending the Folies Bergère, they really were at the Casino de Paris, and when Hitchcock asked to see belly dancing, they were taken to a brothel.[11] They acted, Hitchcock recalled, like "two innocents abroad," whose naïve behavior matched that of their characters.[12]

Because of these resemblances, it is not surprising that the couple in *Rich and Strange* are called Fred (a diminutive of Alfred) and Emily or Em (which evokes Alma). It is, however, surprising that Fred — Hitchcock's surrogate — is from the start self-deceptive, dysfunctional, and petulant. An explanation may lie in the fact that Hitchcock's parents called him "Fred," a name he hated.[13] Thus, his use of the name for this character suggests that Hitchcock created someone who embodied all the aspects of himself that he disliked. The evolution of Fred and of his relationship with Em makes such self-exposure especially courageous, or reckless.

While Fred is seasick, Em meets a fellow passenger, Commander Gordon (Percy Marmont), who shows her a photo of himself seated on the porch of his house, with an empty chair opposite (like the similar empty chair in *The Farmer's Wife*). When she draws in the figure of a woman, this visual detail reveals what is missing in Gordon's life and, unconsciously, what is missing in hers. Em finds it easier to talk to Gordon than to her husband, because he does not intimidate her. "I love Fred and he loves me," she explains, "and, naturally, I want him to think well of me. When I talk to him I'm all so frightened of saying something—foolish. You see, he's terribly clever."

Using Gordon as a sounding board, Em discusses love, calling it "a wonderful thing," which Araminta (in *The Farmer's Wife*) might have said, but Em goes further, describing it in terms that could also apply to Hitchcock's view of travel. Love, she says, "makes everything difficult and dangerous. You know, I don't think love makes people brave, like they say it does in books. I think it makes them timid. I think it makes them frightened when they're happy and sadder when they're sad. You see, everything's multiplied by two—sickness, death, the future. It all means so much more."

After dinner, Em and Gordon stroll on deck. She looks down at the ocean, gets dizzy, and puts her head on his chest. They kiss, and when she pulls away, the off-screen sounds have changed: A sailor's accordion playing has been replaced with arguing voices. This shift in the background sound matches her shift in mood, from quiet and gentle to unsettled and out-of-joint.

Em and Gordon (Percy Marmont) share a romantic moment in *Rich and Strange*.

When Fred finally emerges from his cabin, he is promptly hit in the face with a ring from a game being played on deck. (Larita, in *Easy Virtue*, has an equally fateful encounter when she is hit by John Whittaker's tennis ball.) As usual, Fred's first reaction is irritation, but this does not last. "Fred had met a Princess!"

The Princess (Betty Amann) comes between Fred and Emily during the costume ball.

announces a title, with mock emphasis. Although recovered from his seasickness, Fred remains disoriented, for he falls easy prey to the seductive Princess (Betty Amann).

From here on, Fred and Em interact with each other and, respectively, with the Princess and Gordon. At Port Said, Fred tells Em not to take her camera ashore because it "makes you look like a tourist," as if otherwise they might appear to be natives. (Shortly after, the unselfconscious Gordon asks if he can carry Em's camera for her.) Gazing ashore, Em shares her thoughts with Fred. "To think that place has been there all these years," she says. "All those strange people having their babies, dying, cooking their funny meals. Strange! It's been there all these years!" Fred, oblivious to the honesty of this awkward but insightful realization, snaps back sarcastically, "You don't think they've built it especially for us overnight, do you?" Lacking sensitivity of his own, he has no patience with hers. "You needn't snap my head off," Em replies, adding, "That's the third time you've spoken to me like that since yesterday." Fred is more than usually irritable with Em, because he has become infatuated with the Princess.

The evolving relationships reach a climax during the Carnival, a shipboard dance at which the passengers dress in costume, trying to be people they are not. Gordon tells Em, "I'm drunk," and she replies, "If you are, I am, too." Here, Hitchcock equates inebriation with the disorientation of being attracted to someone one shouldn't. Later, Fred—having had sex with the Princess in her cabin—sits at a table, far more drunk than the others and, by implication, far more disoriented.

At the next port, Em shares a carriage with Gordon and admits, "I'm as much at sea as ever. It's a bewildering business, this being at sea. But, on the night of the Carnival, I knew that Fred and the Princess were—were drunk, too. Compared to them, we were a pair of sobersides." At this point, Hitchcock links the metaphor of being drunk with that of "being at sea," both of which connote a loss of balance. Meanwhile, Fred is with the Princess and she contrasts herself with Em, using a different metaphor. "Having developed a taste for champagne," she asks him, "what's the use of trying to stick to water?" Fred agrees, and asserts, "She never really understood me. I was a bit too much for her." The excursion ashore concludes when Fred and Em, in separate rickshaws, find that their wheels have locked together, and the scene ends with them apart yet inseparable.

On the last night of the cruise, Gordon refers to the picture with the figure Em had drawn and declares his desire to "take care" of her. Separately, the Princess tells Fred, "If a woman can't hold her man, there is no reason why he should take the blame." He responds, "I suppose you're right. You always are." (Like Samuel Sweetland, Fred is easily led, but unlike Sweetland he does not realize it.)

During this voyage, a fellow passenger, Miss Imery (Elsie Randolph), has provided some comic relief, but she also serves thematic functions. An exaggerated reflection of Fred's blindness, this nearsighted spinster wears thick glasses and peers intently at everything and everyone, yet she still has trouble seeing. During the costume ball, she pathetically asks Fred, "Don't you think my shepherdess costume makes me look young?" Fred is disdainful of the unappealing Miss Imery, but his own self-deception runs deeper than hers, for he doesn't just want to look like what he isn't; instead, he believes in his own appeal and puts that belief into action by having sex with the Princess. The difference is also illustrated when Miss Imery asks Fred if he has seen a certain other passenger. The self-absorbed Fred replies, "No," whereupon she discovers the man standing right next to Fred, whose vision problems, we realize, are worse than hers: They are psychological, not physical, and make him feel an inappropriate confidence in his own superiority.

In Singapore, with the first part of their physical and psychological journey over, Em and Fred leave the unsteady sea and go ashore with their respective new partners. Riding in a car, Gordon tells Em the truth about her husband: He is an "empty shell," an "overgrown sham," and "a great baby masquerading as a big, strong man." The Princess, Gordon reveals, is also a fake, "just a common adventuress, and he was the biggest ass aboard." Why didn't he warn Fred, Em asks. "You can't teach the Freds of this world," he replies, with ruthless realism. "When she's spent all his money, she'll drop him like a hot brick." Then, in the film's most extraordinary moment, Em accepts the validity of these statements about Fred, but because of them—not despite them— she decides not to stay with Gordon after all. "A wife's more than half a mother," she explains.

Instead, Em visits the hotel room shared by Fred and the Princess and, after the Princess steps out, tells him that she almost left with Gordon. Fred, blindly hypocritical in his self-absorbed indignation, demands, "How far has this thing gone?" In a direct confrontation, Em shares her new insight into Fred and herself. "He started to show me you as the outside world sees you," she says. "Not as I see you, blinded by love and all this long time together." Although she now realizes that Fred is "a sham" and "a bluff," she chose not to stay with Gordon "*because* I recognize your faults, whereas before I'd always dressed you up in all kinds of silly virtues.... I saw that I was a wife for you. That without me you'd be lost. I couldn't allow that." In *Easy Virtue*, love was akin to pity, but in this film it is linked with both pity and understanding, which lead to sympathy and unselfish support.

When Em reveals that the Princess is "a sham, too," Fred responds with defensive sarcasm — "Is anybody or anything real, then?" — and walks out. Soon, he returns, having learned that the Princess has left him. In anger, he calls the Princess a "fraud," a "little swine," a "streetwalker," and a "tart." Oblivious of his own complicity in his humiliation, he adds, "What a fool she's made of me!" Surprisingly, Em comforts and reinforces Fred. "Yes," she says, "that's what she is. The swine — to treat you like that." Fred now reveals that, on top of everything else, he gave the Princess £1,000, a major part of their funds. Even so, he remains righteous, accusing Em of going off with Gordon. "I didn't," she declares. "Well, did I?" he responds, forgetting that the Princess left *him*.

At this point, it is hard for a viewer to identify with Em's acceptance of Fred, but it also was hard to understand the way Araminta (in *The Farmer's Wife*) and Kate (in *The Manxman*) supported their seriously flawed men. Clearly, in Hitchcock's concept of marriage the wife recognizes her husband's insecurities and helplessness and, knowing that they will not just disappear, permits him to continue his self-deception, a pose required for his survival. If this approach does not fit every marriage, or even most, it contains enough truth to stir healthy self-reflection, and it is so sincerely presented that it probably derives from Hitchcock's own experience.

Writing of his wife in 1956 (in the revealingly titled essay, "The Woman Who Knows Too Much"), Hitchcock said that Alma:

...is most extraordinary in that she's normal.... She has a consistency of presence, a lively personality, a never-clouded expression and she keeps her mouth shut except in magnanimously helpful ways.... She knows that for a thriller-movie-making ogre, I'm hopelessly plebeian and placid.... Next to policemen, I dread being alone. Alma knows that too. I simply like the woman's presence about, even if I'm reading. She puts up with a lot from me.[14]

If Emily Hill is Alma Hitchcock, then *Rich and Strange* depicts her as Hitchcock's ideal woman, someone aware of her husband's flaws and able to support him not despite them, but because of them. And Hitchcock's admiration is believable, because he is willing at the same time to confront his own undesirability.

Fred and Em can still afford a cheap steamer trip home, but if they thought their confrontation at the hotel marked the end of their discoveries, they were wrong. That had been a private matter, but the outside world still has lessons for the couple. When we rejoin them, they are once more "at sea" and their ship suffers a collision. With the cabin door blocked, they are trapped and, faced with seemingly inevitable death, Fred finally drops his pose: He admits to being scared and tells Em, "I'm sorry.... There's only ever been you." She comforts him, and the scene ends as water flows in under the door.

The next morning, however, they are still alive and the deserted ship is partly afloat. They crawl out through a porthole, with Em leading the way to "see if it's all right." No longer faced with immediate death, Fred reverts to his usual self. When Em wonders what caused the accident, he responds, "How the dickens do I know?" and adds, "The silly things you ask!" At this point

Fred and Emily find themselves trapped on a sinking ship.

Hitchcock has, without being obvious about it, created a thoroughly appropriate metaphor for the Hills' marriage: They share a sinking ship—or, as a title aptly phrases it, a "drifting derelict."

Soon, a Chinese junk pulls alongside. As men swarm aboard to scavenge, Fred and Em climb onto the junk, carrying a cat they have rescued. The men then return with their plunder, ignoring the intruders. One of them gets his foot caught in a rope, which lowers him head first into the sea while the others stare, making no move to help. Hitchcock's close shots of Fred and Em watching this recall similar close-ups used in Paris, but this time the shots convey grim sobriety, not giddy exuberance. That encounter was with landmarks; now, as their old life sinks behind them, they encounter bewildering human realities.

A pregnant Chinese woman brings them food, which they devour hungrily. "Not half as bad as people make out," says Em of the meal. "Nothing ever is," responds Fred, smugly. Shortly after, a man emerges from the cabin and nails the cat's skin to a wall to dry. Fred and Em, realizing what they have eaten, head for the boat's railing.

Later, hearing a newborn baby's cry, Em says, "Isn't it wonderful!" but Fred only declares, "These darn Chinese breed like rabbits." As the baby is brought on deck, he adds, "Isn't it ugly!" Someone fills a pail with sea water to throw on the baby, which Em tries to stop, because a newborn could not survive the shock. Fred urges her not to intrude. Here, at the climax of their journey, Fred and Em have come face to face with the essence of existence: death, birth, and the impenetrability of alien perspectives.

Upon returning home, Fred and Em reveal few signs of change. Their radio reports that the "channel crossing's extremely rough," a reminder of their experiences, but they don't discuss the matter. Fred wonders whether a baby carriage would fit through the hallway. Em declares, "When you get your new job as traveler for the firm, I'm going to a bigger, better house than this." But Fred doesn't want to move. "We've been here all these years," he says. She responds, "That's one of the very reasons why —" and the film ends as they bicker. In such an epilogue, a traditional film would have summarized the lessons learned by the couple, but Hitchcock provides only hints, forcing viewers to work harder than they may wish.

Of the few critics who have analyzed the ending of *Rich and Strange*, some conclude that Fred and Em retreat to the security of their old relationship; others claim that the two have changed for the better. Hitchcock, however, refuses to satisfy our desire for an easy conclusion, and his final scene implies a combination of both viewpoints.

Yes, Fred and Em bicker at the film's end, but oblivious bickering is different from bickering with a grasp of what underlies their personalities and relationship. Yes, disturbing insights have been gained, but daily life requires an illusion of security. Yes, Fred remains what he always was, even while he considers starting a family, for although he knows more about himself than he did, he cannot alter his nature. Yes, Em supports Fred in his weakness and vulnerability, but she now understands his nature, instead of creating a fantasy version of it. She also adopts a new assertiveness, which contains the threat of independence ("*I'm* going to a bigger, better house"). This challenging last scene is consistent with the rest of the work, and Hitchcock is all the more courageous for his refusal to simplify matters.

Em and Fred are still bickering at the end of *Rich and Strange*.

Rich and Strange is Hitchcock's most personal revelation to date, with its characters and relationships emerging naturally from his prior films. Its shipboard romantic triangle stems from *Champagne*, except that the earlier film's heroine, loyal boyfriend, and sophisticated man who is not what he seems have become the hero, loyal wife, and sophisticated woman who is not what she seems. In *Easy Virtue* and *The Ring*, the woman marries a naïve and limited man, and in *The Ring* she is tempted by a worldly, attentive outsider. The complaint of Samuel Sweetland, in *The Farmer's Wife*, that women "have taken away my self-respect," anticipates Fred's statement that the Princess had made a fool of him. Sweetland, however, admits his limitations and humbles himself to 'Minta, whereas Fred never quite reaches that point, which contributes to the uncompromising tone of *Rich and Strange*.

The Manxman dealt with two self-centered men—one blind and helpless, the other selfishly egocentric—who are linked by friendship and a shared love of Kate. Jack and Bob in *The Ring* echo this arrangement, in a muted fashion, as do the males in *The Lodger* (Joe and the lodger), *Champagne* (the father and the boyfriend), and *Blackmail* (Frank and the artist). *Rich and Strange* turns this pair of characters into one individual, Fred, who is both blind and selfish, helpless and egocentric. As a result, Em must come to terms with both sets of qualities, sympathizing with one, while understanding and accepting the other, just as 'Minta does regarding Sweetland in *The Farmer's Wife*.

Hitchcock anticipated the structural pattern of *Rich and Strange* by dividing *Downhill* into three sections, each introduced with a title: "The World of Youth," "The World of Make Believe," and "The World of Lost Illusions." These stages of Roddy's journey parallel Fred's evolution, which moves from the security of predictable activity to a world of make-believe on the cruise. Then, in Singapore and after, Fred loses his illusions. The circular structure of *Rich and Strange* also has precedents: *Easy Virtue* opens and closes with a divorce case, *The Ring* starts and ends with a boxing match, and in *The Farmer's Wife* Sweetland leaves 'Minta and the farm, only to return to both. In *Downhill*, Roddy—like Fred—returns home and his life seems little changed, but (as Maurice Yacowar points out) Roddy is "no longer bewildered by the sordid realities beyond" his familiar existence.[15] Fred, too, carries on a life over which will hover an ever-present, but unverbalized, awareness derived from his experience in the outer world.

Even Hitchcock's use of subjective shots in *Rich and Strange* fits his evolving style. In most of his silent films, the meaning implied by such shots is clear, but in *Blackmail* he went an important step further. Near the end, when Alice goes to Scotland Yard to give herself up, she asks to see the inspector and, while waiting, gazes outside. Here, Hitchcock offers not a subjective multiple exposure but a simple shot of traffic passing. Under other circumstances, this image would be nondescript, but because Alice expects to be arrested it takes on subtly sensitive overtones as a last view of what she expects will soon be lost to her, while evoking the irony that life carries on despite her plight.

In *Rich and Strange*, Hitchcock twice employs this kind of reserved subjectivity. When Em rides in a car with Gordon and hears the truth about Fred and the Princess, she looks down at the road as it rushes by, which conveys her sense of being carried away by events. Later, after she confronts Fred in the hotel room and he walks out, Em sits down, crying, and stares past the two vertical bars of a window at palm trees and the ocean, as the voice of a native singer is heard. This shot creates a calm mood, but one from which Em is presently cut off. In these two cases, Hitchcock uses images compellingly, but their emotional overtones are so subtle that they run the risk of ambiguity.

In filming this valentine to Alma, Hitchcock also painted a very unflattering self-portrait. By publicly acknowledging his flaws and his need of Alma's support, Hitchcock achieved something that his negative alter ego, Fred, could not. He also took several stylistic and dramatic chances, and so made himself vulnerable both personally and professionally. Therefore, he was especially distressed when the critics and the public didn't like his film and, what is worse, didn't understand it.

Hitchcock never acknowledged the confessional quality of *Rich and Strange*, but although in later years he usually voiced agreement with critics and audiences, he faithfully defended this film, asserting that "it had lots of ideas.... I liked the picture; it should have been more successful."[16] In 1935, he probably had *Rich and Strange* in mind when he wrote that if

> ...a producer is offering the public
> something which may be unwelcome

> or indigestible to it, stars are of the utmost value as camouflage — or, if you prefer it, as the jam round the pill.[17]

Nearly 30 years later, he declared:

> My mistake with *Rich and Strange*, was my failure to make sure that the two leading players would be attractive to the critics and audience alike.[18]

Certainly, the appeal of a Robert Donat or Michael Redgrave would have counterbalanced Fred's negative qualities — a function served by Cary Grant in *Suspicion* (1941) and *Notorious* (1946) and by James Stewart in *Vertigo* (1958) — but one can argue that Henry Kendall's charmlessness as Fred challenges viewers to consider Em's acceptance of him more thoroughly.

At the time of its release, *Rich and Strange* derailed Hitchcock's career. He and B.I.P. severed their six-year relationship and Hitchcock did not direct again until *Waltzes from Vienna* (1933), a musical about the creative conflict between Johann Strauss, Sr. (Edmund Gwenn), who writes music in an orderly, traditional fashion, and his son (Esmond Knight), who composes out of a burning compulsion. The struggle between these artists' creative philosophies can be seen to represent the two sides of a debate that must have been raging within Hitchcock himself. His attraction to this aspect is suggested by the fact that, according to a contemporary interviewer, Hitchcock was hired only to supervise the film and the "step from that to actually directing it was taken because the subject interested Hitchcock so much."[19]

The tensions within Hitchcock affected the production atmosphere, and his leads found working with him an unpleasant experience. At one point, Hitchcock reportedly declared, "I hate

In France, *Waltzes from Vienna* was retitled *The Song of the Danube*.

this sort of stuff." (Spoto, 136) Years later, he called this period "my lowest ebb" (Bogdanovich, 16) and a time when he engaged in "a thoroughly sobering self-examination."[20]

CHAPTER SIX

HITCHCOCK BECOMES "HITCHCOCK"

> "I *know* that art must first of all be
> commercially popular
> to be successful."
> — Alfred Hitchcock[1]

At the end of *Waltzes from Vienna*, the public applauds the music of the younger Strauss, music that the establishment had disdained, and the film's director must have wished for a similar conclusion to his own creative efforts. The man who, in 1926, had decided to cultivate the critics now felt that they had failed him when he needed them most. So, Hitchcock took a leaf from Strauss's book and, in a 1933 interview, declared his intention to make

> ...popular pictures which anybody can understand. But without being highbrow, I believe in making them in such a way that they will appeal to the most intelligent people as well.[2]

Three decades later, Hitchcock put this decision in perspective. He said:

> You see, when a director has been let down by the critics, when he feels that his work has been passed on too

Waltzes from Vienna is a musical about the creative conflict between Johann Strauss, Sr. and his son. (Photofest)

lightly, his only recourse is to seek recognition via the public. Of course, if a filmmaker thinks solely in box office terms, he will wind up doing routine stuff, and that's bad, too.[3]

Hitchcock chose to appeal to the public, rather than the critics—to be entertaining, rather than serious—but he would do so on his own terms, without prostituting himself or significantly compromising his work. How could he achieve that goal?

As a first step in that direction, he responded to the popularity of the few crime films he had made. After all, most of his other pictures—including *Rich and Strange*—had also been concerned with revealing human psychology through stressful situations. Also, he had always been interested in real-life criminal trials, and such material offered an ideal opportunity to create carefully calculated "entertainments" that might be enjoyed only on that level, but that might also include thematic and character insights beyond what is expected from suspense thrillers. By 1948 he had accepted the suspense thriller as ideal for his purposes. "Within its framework," he explained, "I can tell any story under the sun."[4]

Hitchcock could not have anticipated specializing in such films when he conceived *The Man Who Knew Too Much* (1934). He was, after all, only trying to re-establish his position in the industry. A lucky encounter with his former producer, the supportive Michael Balcon, brought an offer to make the film for his company, and Ivor Montagu, the friend who had helped revise *The Lodger*, added to the positive atmosphere by serving as associate producer. When *The Man Who Knew Too Much* was released, as part of a double feature, it scored a resounding success.

However, Hitchcock's old nemesis, C.M. Woolf, still controlled distribution. As Montagu recalled, he "did not like either of us" and so "made up his books the *opposite* way, to record ours as the second of the two [features], with the result that, although the film had cost only about £40,000 it showed a heavy loss. He then made this the excuse to sack both of us, while in temporary charge of the studio during the absence of the producer Michael Balcon, in America." Balcon returned "just in time to re-sign us and reinstate" their next picture, which became *The 39 Steps*.[5]

The Man Who Knew Too Much achieved Hitchcock's goal, but it also reinforced his suspicion of industry "experts" like Woolf. The critics, too, while enthusiastic, revealed their limitations. According to *Kinematograph Weekly*,[6] "Alfred Hitchcock has obviously learnt by past experience that real money lies only in mass appeal, and with this wise thought in his mind he has

Ramon (Frank Vosper, left), with Abbott (Peter Lorre) and Nurse Agnes (Cicely Oates), defend themselves in *The Man Who Knew Too Much*. (Photofest)

given us a picture of first-class melodrama."[7]   This critic clearly preferred what he assumed to be a simple melodrama over a more ambitious film, such as *Rich and Strange*.

If everything depended on the acceptance of his films by the public, then Hitchcock would cultivate the public as assiduously as he had the critics in the past. He began to publish chatty, but informative, articles under his byline in newspapers and popular film magazines, as a way of connecting with the public, keeping them aware of his name, and educating them about his medium. (Eighteen of Hitchcock's 1933-39 essays, plus others, are reprinted in the invaluable anthology, *Hitchcock on Hitchcock*.)

In keeping with his new determination to appear to entertain, Hitchcock modified his use of film technique. If formal experimentation had contributed to the public's disinterest in *Rich and Strange*, then he would dispense with it. In 1936, Hitchcock published an apology for his earlier, more extreme uses of the medium. He wrote:

> I played about with "technique" in those early days. I tried crazy tricks with violent cuts, dissolves, and wipes with everything in the room spinning round and standing on its head.... I have stopped all that today. I have not the film time to throw away on fancy stuff. I like my screen well used, with every corner filled, but no arty theories clamping the action down. Nowadays I want the cutting and continuity to be as inconspicuous as possible, and all I am concerned with is to get the characters developed and the story clearly told without any directorial idiosyncrasies.[8]

He restated this position in 1937, writing that:

> ...in recent years I have come to make much less use of obvious camera devices. I have become more commercially minded; afraid that anything at all subtle may be missed. ...nowadays I try to tell a story in the simplest possible way, so that I can feel sure it will hold the attention of any audience and won't puzzle them.[9]

This became a constant refrain.

The "new" Hitchcock worked hard to convince everyone that he had become a simpler, less ambitious filmmaker. But his ambitions remained, as did his subject matter and his integrated use of film technique. Hitchcock merely became devious. The thriller form offered strong plot lines and equally strong emotions that would hold the attention of viewers, and to help them identify with his protagonists, he centered on ordinary people caught up in extraordinary circumstances (much like Fred and Em in *Rich and Strange*).

The result is a film less about events than about people affected by events, with a plot that could easily have been turned into a standard drama, while the thriller aspect hooks a viewer's interest and *seems* to be the film's reason for existence. At his best, the "new" Hitchcock intertwines story and character so thoroughly that the thriller aspects are inseparable from the psychological and thematic ones. Precedent for this can be seen in *The Lodger*, where the policeman who suspects the title character of killing young blondes is also the suitor of a young blonde with whom the lodger develops a relationship. Thus, although any policeman might have suspected the lodger under any circumstances, this man's suspicion relates directly to his personal involvement, his jealousy.

Because Hitchcock sought to discard the more "experimental" use of visual (and aural) images to reveal a character's inner state, it was even more necessary for his plot's concrete details to serve as metaphors that communicate psychological and emotional meanings. In the process, Hitchcock gravitated to thriller situations bearing remarkable similarities to those in his mainstream films.

For example, in *Easy Virtue*, a worldly woman with a secret in her past meets and marries a naïve young man in the south of France who then brings her to his English home, where she feels like an intruder and is intimidated by his domineering mother. This story hardly suggests a suspense thriller, yet in Daphne du Maurier's novel, *Rebecca*, Hitchcock found its counterpart: A worldly man with a secret in his past meets and marries a naïve young woman in the south of France. He then brings her to his English home, where she feels like an intruder and is intimidated by his domineering housekeeper. By the same token, *Easy Virtue*'s link between press photographers and the destruction of Larita's life reaches a climax after her second divorce, when she tells some cameramen, "Shoot! There's nothing left to kill." Years later, in *Foreign Correspondent* (1940), Hitchcock would include a literal version of that metaphor when an assassin, disguised as a press photographer, holds a pistol next to his camera, aims both, and kills a public figure.

The Man Who Knew Too Much reveals Hitchcock's use of thriller material to tell a story about people. In it, a child is kidnapped to prevent her parents from divulging information about a planned assassination. While developing that situation—saving the politician and rescuing the child—Hitchcock reveals much of what was also on his mind when he made *Rich and Strange*. As before, aspects of the married couple have an autobiographical basis. The Hitchcocks had honeymooned in St. Moritz, Switzerland, and they often returned on their anniversary, accompanied by their daughter. *The Man Who Knew Too Much* opens in St. Moritz, where a British family—Bob and Jill Lawrence, and their daughter, Betty—are on vacation, oblivious of the real nature of the world. Also as before, the married couple has relationship problems, and physical danger is both a threat to the characters' well-being and a challenge that modifies their personalities, bringing the domestic unit closer.

In *The Man Who Knew Too Much*, Hitchcock devotes considerable time to introducing his characters. At first, the Lawrences seem to be in harmony, to possess a relaxed and balanced understanding, as they banter together. However, Hitchcock implies that more seethes below the couple's good-humored surface than even they realize. Before long, alert viewers can conclude that Bob and Jill are childlike, willful, and shallow, although in different ways.

In the first scene, Bob and Betty (Leslie Banks and Nova Pilbeam) stand on the sidelines, watching ski jumpers. When the dog she is holding breaks free and runs into the skiers' path, Betty impulsively chases it, which causes a skier to fall. Other people are also knocked down, including Abbott (Peter Lorre), who is accompanied by Nurse Agnes. The skier is Louis (Pierre Fresnay), a man whom the Lawrences already know. Although the accident was potentially life threatening, Bob and Betty are all laughs and giggles afterward.

After Louis mentions that he will be leaving that night, Bob says, "We shall miss you" and Betty chimes in with, "Mommy will cry her eyes out. Won't she, daddy?" Bob, adopting an exaggeratedly hen-pecked tone, says, "Yes, dear." Louis asks, "You think so?" and Betty replies, "Oh, she adores you. Doesn't she, daddy?" Bob then repeats, in the same tone, "Yes, dear." Already, we can sense unacknowledged dissension between the taciturn Bob and his wife, whom we have not yet met. Louis invites the Lawrences to dinner and, when Betty asks to stay up late and join them, Bob — seemingly out of habit — evades the decision, saying, "Ask your mother."

In the next scene, Bob and Betty are again on the sidelines, watching Jill (Edna Best) compete in the finals of clay pigeon shooting. Her rival is Ramon (Frank Vosper), whom Bob has just naïvely described as a "bit of a bore, but he means well." Betty, however, dislikes Ramon, and her judgment will prove better than her parents'. Jill's aim is thrown off by the sound of Abbott's chiming watch, when he shows it to Betty, and she blames the girl for her miss. In Betty's presence, Jill and Bob speak of her in the third person, as "your child," and Jill declares, "If I lose this game, I'll disown it forever." Jill also tells Ramon, "Let that be a lesson to you — never have any children," while Bob playfully kicks Betty in the rear and calls her "fat-head." None of this seems to bother Betty, but real feelings are being expressed here, in the guise of joking banter.

When Louis enters, Jill and he embrace and exchange exaggerated endearments. Then, as Jill walks off with Louis, her arm around his neck, she tells her husband, "You can keep your brat! I'm going off with another man!" Bob puts a handkerchief to his face and pretends to sob, whereupon Jill tells her husband to "go to bed early, with Betty," as if he, too, were a child. "Poor

daddy," says Betty, and the viewer is likely to agree, despite the scene's mood of cheerful teasing.

That evening, in the dining room, Bob and Betty sit at a table, like obedient children, while the adults, Jill and Louis, dance. When Jill maneuvers Louis next to the table, they engage in a mock conversation for her husband's benefit. "What do you think of the average Englishman?" Louis asks, to which Jill replies, "Much too cold!" Bob then asks if the sweater Jill has been knitting is for Louis. "Of course it is," she replies, tauntingly. "You think it was for you?" To Louis, she adds, "It's a memento." Louis plays along, responding with mock passion, "To wear over my beating heart!"

Bob attaches the end of the yarn to Louis's jacket, so that as he dances off with Jill, the sweater gradually unravels, with yarn looping around the other couples. When the sweater has almost disappeared, Louis realizes that something is wrong, stops dancing, and looks down. A bullet is fired through a window. Louis shifts his gaze in that direction, then at Jill, and then down at a small spot on his chest. "Oh, look," he says with understated surprise, and slowly collapses to the floor. As he dies, he gives Jill his room key and whispers a message. This leads Bob to find a cryptic note hidden in Louis's shaving brush, but the criminals learn he has it and kidnap Betty to keep her parents quiet.

Peter Lorre as Abbott in a posed shot from *The Man Who Knew Too Much*.

From the start, the banter of Bob and Jill cuts too close to the bone for comfort, and by the time of the dancing, the jokes sound like barely disguised cruelty. As a result, although Bob's trick with the yarn seems harmless, it suggests a real (if unstated) jealousy of Louis and a resentment at Jill's taunting. In addition, by placing this action where he does, Hitchcock contrasts its mundane silliness, Jill's casual ruthlessness, and Bob's immature passivity with something truly serious—a death. The yarn incident also establishes an image that fits the way the film's opening scenes introduce all the major characters: Louis, whose death sets the plot in motion; the three Lawrences; and their three antagonists, Ramon, Abbott, and Agnes. The paths of all these people intersect in much the same chance way that the meandering tangle of yarn links the dancing strangers.

These initial encounters are filled with anticipatory irony, which underlines how little anyone knows about the future. Apologizing to the man who will soon have him killed, Louis tells Abbott, "Sorry I upset you." He tells Betty that he could have been killed in the ski accident, adding that "my last day here might have been my last day on earth." Jill's dialogue with Ramon, the future assassin, also hints at what will come. "Sworn enemies, eh?" she says jokingly, and after her loss she comments, "We must have another battle one day." Ramon replies, "I shall live for that moment," a moment that, it turns out, will bring his death. This suggestion of future events is another instance of Hitchcock's circular plot structure. In *The Ring*, Jack lost his first contest with Bob, but defeats him in a rematch. Here, Jill loses the shooting contest with Ramon but, in the climax, triumphs when Ramon pursues Betty onto a roof and she shoots the man who had defeated her.

The Lawrences may be bystanders, but they are not quite innocent ones. What happens to them serves as a kind of punishment for their flippant approach to human relations. The villains, after all, do not tell Bob that they will kill Betty, only that he "will never see" his child again, which would make good Jill's joking threat to "disown" Betty "forever."

Rich and Strange exists to show the evolution of Fred and Em, but *The Man Who Knew Too Much* must seem to exist for its dramatic plot, so Hitchcock has more difficulty establishing a change in Bob and Jill. Nonetheless, change does occur. Initially, Bob is passive and childlike, but when presented with a crisis he takes the initiative by investigating the clues left by Louis. "Our only chance is to act ourselves," he declares, and so he and Uncle Clive (another adult child, who plays with the train set he gave Betty) are forced to act like adults. Although Bob is ultimately captured, he breaks free, releases his daughter, and gets her onto the roof.

But it is Jill who foils the assassination during a concert and later saves Betty. Her change is shown through the contrast between her two encounters with Ramon. The first time, she loses because she is distracted (she thinks) by her daughter. In the climax, that daughter is being threatened and could be an even greater

Jill and Bob Lawrence (Edna Best and Leslie Banks) worry about their daughter in *The Man Who Knew Too Much.* **(Photofest)**

distraction, but this time Jill maintains her composure. Significantly, when Jill fires at Ramon, Hitchcock shows her face, not the rifle, which reveals that his interest lies more in the person than the event. By encountering chaos and standing up to it, Jill matures; she learns how to do more than play, by replacing her aimless energy with self-discipline. The irresponsible looseness of Bob and Jill turns into teamwork, as each contributes to the happy ending. The final shot is, appropriately, of the three family members united in an embrace (although one might wish for an epilogue that would reveal their new selves).

The Man Who Knew Too Much lends itself to Hitchcock's already-familiar view of life as an obstacle course composed of

Bob struggles with a dangerous dentist (Henry Oscar) in *The Man Who Knew Too Much.*

ambiguous perceptions and faulty vision. Objects, places, people, and even words often disguise their meanings, which leads to blurred distinctions and false assumptions. Louis's shaving brush hides an important message, but that message is itself ambiguous, with "A. Hall" assumed to be a person's name, whereas it refers to the Albert Hall. In conversation, words become confused and their meanings elusive, as when Abbott, asked if he is all right after the ski accident, replies, "My English isn't good enough to know," or when Bob fails to communicate with a German-speaking policeman, in an exchange filled with wordplay ("*herr*," "hair," "here").

Paradoxically, the entrance of Bob and Clive into the "real" world requires that they start playing roles. In the office of a menacing dentist, both men pretend to have toothaches and Bob claims to be a sailor just off a ship. After a short struggle, Bob switches places

Nova Pilbeam, Leslie Banks and Edna Best in *The Man Who Knew Too Much*

with the dentist, putting on his white coat and glasses. Then, to keep the plotters from seeing him well enough to detect the pose, Bob aims a light at the door and the glare obscures the vision of anyone entering.

The Tabernacle of the Sun, where a grandmotherly old lady pulls out a pistol, is a front for anarchist-murderers, and when Clive arrives with a policeman, Abbott revises the officer's perception and has Clive arrested for "disorderly behavior in a sacred edifice." At the Albert Hall, a drama is enacted not so much behind the scenes as beneath the surface, without the concert audience realizing it. The anarchists monitor the assassination by listening to a radio broadcast of the concert and conclude from what they hear that Ramon succeeds. "Sounds as if it went off all right," one of them says, and the film's viewers are led to think the same, because of what Hitchcock chooses to show and not to show.

In terms of film technique, Hitchcock did not completely drop the use of subjective distortion, despite his public claims. As Jill faints after learning about the kidnapping, Hitchcock dissolves from her face to a swish pan of the room, and when Nurse Agnes hypnotizes Clive, there is a subjectively hazy shot of her face. During the concert, Jill's view of the chorus and orchestra goes out of focus, matching her loss of concentration. On other occasions, though, Hitchcock's technique is unobtrusively expressive. After Bob burns a note from the kidnappers, the director dissolves from the flames to a close-up of a pin worn by Betty, so for a few seconds it is engulfed by fire, dramatizing her danger. Later, at the Albert Hall, Ramon hands Jill the same pin and, as she sits in the audience, whenever she glances at the object we understand her train of thought.

Jill screams during the Albert Hall sequence of *The Man Who Knew Too Much* **(Photofest)**

The five-minute sequence of Jill at the concert hall is almost entirely wordless, with Hitchcock linking superficially unrelated shots so that the viewer grasps their implied relationship and significance. Each image communicates very little meaning on its own; instead, the meaning exists in the viewers' minds, as they draw conclusions from the juxtaposition of one shot with the next. For example, at one point, Hitchcock cuts from a microphone to a radio and then to the anarchists in their hideout, and the viewer understands that the concert is being broadcast and the anarchists are listening. The sequence's climax, constructed in this fashion, intercuts separate close shots of a gun barrel, the victim, and Jill's face.

In such situations, we see the result of a partial shift in Hitchcock's allegiance from German Expressionism to the kind of editing found in the Soviet films of the 1920s. It was at the London Film Society that Hitchcock first encountered the editing style of such directors as V.I. Pudovkin, whose writings about the medium attracted the Society's attention. In fact, Hitchcock's friend, Ivor Montagu, translated one of Pudovkin's essays, which was published in London in October 1928.

In that essay, Pudovkin compared editing to a writer's use of words. A film, he explained, is

> built up from the separate strips of celluloid that are its raw material. If a writer requires a word—for example, *beech*—the single word is only the raw skeleton of a meaning, so to speak, a concept without essence or precision. Only in conjunction with other words, set in the frame of a complex form, does art endow it with life and reality.... I claim that every object, taken from a given viewpoint and shown on the screen to spectators, is a *dead object*, even though it has moved before the camera. The proper movement of an object before the camera is yet no movement on the screen, it is no more than raw material for the future building-up, by editing, of the movement that is conveyed by the assemblage of the various strips of film. Only if the object be placed together among a number of separate objects, only if it be presented as part of a synthesis of different separate visual images, is it endowed with filmic life.[10]

Hitchcock may have been aware of Pudovkin's views before the publication of this essay, because in his November 1927 letter to the *London Evening News* he used a similar analogy, referring to "the nouns, verbs, and adjectives of the film language."

On February 3, 1929, Pudovkin delivered a lecture in London at a Film Society meeting and if Hitchcock didn't attend he probably read the text, which was published soon after. On this occasion, Pudovkin described an editing experiment on which he had assisted his mentor, Lev Kuleshov.

> We took from some film or other several close-ups of the well-known Russian actor Mosjukhin. We chose close-ups which were static and which did not express any feeling at all — quiet close-ups. We joined these close-ups, which were all similar, with other bits of film in three different combinations. In the first combination the close-up of Mosjukhin was immediately followed by a shot of a plate of soup standing on a table. It was obvious and certain that Mosjukhin was looking at this soup. In the second combination the face of Mosjukhin was joined to shots showing a coffin in which lay a dead woman. In the third the close-up was followed by a shot of a little girl playing with a funny toy bear. When we showed the three combinations to an audience which had not been let into the secret the result was terrific. The public raved about the acting of the artist. They pointed out the heavy pensiveness of his mood over the forgotten soup, were touched and moved by the deep sorrow with which he looked on the dead woman, and admired the light, happy smile with which he surveyed the girl at play. But

we knew that in all three cases the face was exactly the same.[11]

Thus, the viewer's impression of a char-acter's thought or feeling owes less to the actor's performance than to the indication, through editing, of what that character is seeing and, by implication, thinking. Hitchcock had used this technique in *The Farmer's*

Wife in the scene where Samuel Sweetland looked at his wedding picture and then the empty chair, but generally he had revealed thoughts in the more stylized German manner, through distorted images and multiple exposures. But now, seeking to avoid such visual self-consciousness, he found Pudovkin's approach to be a rewarding cinematic alternative, as in the concert hall sequence of *The Man Who Knew Too Much*.

Hitchcock's commitment to Pudovkin's principles is evident in his essays. In 1937, he wrote:

> What I like to do always is to photograph just the little bits of a scene that I really need for building up a visual sequence. I want to put my film together on the screen, not simply to photograph something that has been put together already, [and to treat a scene] as a piece of raw material which must be broken up, taken to bits, before it can be woven into an expressive visual pattern.[12]

For the rest of his life, Hitchcock continued to advocate Pudovkin's principles. In 1963, he even described the editing of shots showing James Stewart in *Rear Window* (1954) in a way that paraphrases Pudovkin's account of the Mosjukhin experiment:

> Mr. Stewart looks out. Close-up. Cut
> to what he sees. Let's assume it's a
> woman holding a baby in her arms. Cut
> back to him. He smiles. Mr. Stewart
> likes babies. He's a nice gentleman.
> Take out only the middle piece of
> film, the viewpoint. Leave the close-
> ups in—the look and the smile. Put a
> nude girl in the middle instead of the
> baby. Now he's a dirty old man. By
> the changing of one piece of film only,
> you change the whole idea.[13]

Hitchcock's response to the failure of *Rich and Strange* altered his career, but he was incapable of retreating into the glib superficiality that critics and the public seemed to seek. Although he modified his narrative approach and visual style in *The Man Who Knew Too Much* and the films that followed, he continued to draw on some very personal interests and retained his commitment to film as a subtle medium of expression.

Squire Pengallan (Charles Laughton) finds out "just how far you can go," in *Jamaica Inn* (1939).

CHAPTER SEVEN

KNOWING HOW FAR YOU CAN GO

"The art of directing for the
commercial market
is to know just how
far you can go."
— Alfred Hitchcock[1]

Hitchcock consolidated the gains he had made with *The Man Who Knew Too Much* in his next film, *The 39 Steps* (1935), which proved so successful that it even had an impact on the United States market. Not surprisingly, this happened despite the efforts of C.M. Woolf, who had initially canceled the project as "too highbrow."[2] The film, however, is the epitome of humorous and exciting entertainment.

The plot of *The 39 Steps* is set in motion by an event quite similar to that in *The Man Who Knew Too Much*: A traveler (a Canadian in London, this time) encounters a charming foreigner (a woman, this time) who turns out to be a secret agent; the agent is killed, but before dying she gives the man information about an enemy plot. Like the Lawrences, this hero, Richard Hannay (Robert Donat), starts to investigate on his own. In John Buchan's 1915 novel, *The 39 Steps*, an enemy intends to disrupt Europe by assassinating a foreign politician during a visit to London. Hitchcock had borrowed that situation for *The Man Who Knew Too Much*, so he changed his new film's premise to the need to keep a defense secret from leaving England. The Lawrences had been motivated by fear for their daughter's welfare, but Hannay finds himself in a different, if no less distressing, predicament: He is suddenly threatened by both the police, who suspect him of murder, and the enemy agents.

The 39 Steps retains the spontaneous feeling of *The Man Who Knew Too Much*, but adds high polish and efficiency. The plot, moving at a rapid pace, contains not a wasted moment, yet has room for resonant details, interesting secondary characters, and numerous twists and surprises. As a consequence, it generally lacks the double level of storytelling found in *The Man Who Knew Too Much*. Here, the plot often exists for the events themselves, instead of for the insights into the characters implied by those events. Hannay is not initially flawed, he reveals no complexity, nor is he appreciably changed by his experiences. He has no middle-class complacency or self-satisfied parochialism to be disrupted, nor does he have a wife or daughter to take for granted or who misunderstand him.

In fact, Hitchcock has so little interest in his hero's everyday life and personality that he introduces Hannay as an unidentified figure (in shots of just his hands and feet) who buys a ticket to a music hall show and enters. We do not see his face—i.e., meet him as an individual—until he emerges from the crowd by asking a question of the performer, Mr. Memory. Soon after, a shot is fired, the audience rushes out, and in the confusion an attractive stranger (Lucie Mannheim) invites herself to his rooms, where she is killed.

Thus Hitchcock plunges directly into the story's dramatic, amusing, and romantic events. He also implies that Hannay is of no significance until pulled from his mundane existence, which isn't worth depicting, and confronted with the dangerous, unpredictable aspects of the world that he never realized existed around him. At the same time, by starting and ending the narrative in a theater (which the novel did not do), Hitchcock suggests that his film is just an entertainment staged for our benefit.

The on-stage death of Mr. Memory (Wylie Watson) in *The 39 Steps* **(1935). (Photofest)**

Indeed, Hannay finds that becoming a part of the "real" world is like participating in a show, one in which little can be taken at face value and one that forces him to improvise a series of performances. This process may not punish him or teach him a lesson about himself, but Hannay does learn to dissimulate effectively, and he gains some experience discovering truths about others. Ironically, Mr. Memory's act, which opens and closes the film, involves answering questions, providing accurate facts—in short, telling the truth. When Hannay leaves the theater, he enters a world in which lies may be more convincing than the truth, and sometimes more accurate.

Although *The 39 Steps* is full of misinterpretations, both verbal and visual, meanings are so undependable that at times a

Hannay (Robert Donat), a fake politician, is arrested by fake policemen as Pamela (Madeleine Carroll) watches in *The 39 Steps*. (Photofest)

deliberate lie or flirtatious joke cuts surprisingly close to the bone. For example, when Hannay asks the woman outside the theater if she is an actress, she replies, "Not in the way you mean," which states the truth but fails to reveal it. She then asks to go home with him. "Well, it's your funeral," he jokes. Later, on a train, a lingerie salesman looks up from his newspaper and declares, "Is there no *honesty* in this world at all?" He is not, however, referring to Hannay's deception, but to the fact that a corset is being sold at a price lower than his.

To convince a milkman to help him escape from his own apartment house, Hannay fails with the truth but succeeds when he claims to be eluding his lover's husband. Later, at the home of a Scottish tenant farmer, or crofter, he claims to be a mechanic-chauffeur. At the same time, the grimly religious crofter (John Laurie, who played Johnny in *Juno and the Paycock*) is willing to hide Hannay from the police for money, after which he betrays him for more money.

Not long after, Hannay assumes that Professor Jordan (Godfrey Tearle) is a pillar of the community and a man to be trusted, only to discover that he leads the enemy spy ring. As Jordan explains, "My whole existence will be jeopardized if it became known that I am not—what shall we say?—not what I seem." At this point, Jordan shoots Hannay, or so it seems, but Hannay is saved by a hymnal in a pocket of the crofter's jacket he is wearing. Hannay next tells the truth to the local sheriff, who pretends to believe him until the police enter and arrest Hannay, who plunges through a window and pretends to be part of a passing temperance parade.

When Hannay slips into a meeting hall, he is welcomed as the late-arriving politician for whom the audience was waiting, so the man who wants to hide becomes the center of attention. Faking a speech, he ends up speaking the truth. "I know what it's like to feel lonely and helpless and have the whole world against me," he declares, with passion. (In the novel, Hannay gave a speech at the candidate's request, but Hitchcock turned that situation into this one, which far more fully reflects his interests.) Hannay gets an ovation from the listeners, who have responded to the emotional honesty behind his pose. When Hannay is arrested, his audience thinks he is being given an escort and continue applauding. Before long, though, he realizes that the supposed officers are in fact henchmen of Professor Jordan.

Now, chance again crosses Hannay's path with that of Pamela (Madeleine Carroll), whom he first met on the train to Scotland, and when he flees this time they are handcuffed together. Unlike Bob and Jill Lawrence in *The Man Who Knew Too Much*, these two meet for the first time during the story, which makes *The 39 Steps* a tale of courtship, not a re-evaluation of an established relationship. Nevertheless, the subject of marriage—and people's attitudes toward it—permeates the film, often through its secondary characters.

"You married?" Hannay asks the milkman early on. "Yes," he replies, "but don't rub it in." A little later, on the train, a picture

Pamela and Hannay, handcuffed together, flee both the police and the spies in *The 39 Steps*. (Photofest)

of an old-fashioned corset reminds a lingerie salesman of his wife and he shudders. The film's crofter sequence elaborates on what, in the book, was a very limited encounter. Here, the couple is so mismatched that Hannay assumes the man's wife (Peggy Ashcroft) is his daughter. She, unlike her husband, is interested in city life and the possibility of having fun, but she also accepts her present joyless life.

As the crofter says grace before dinner, he refers to "us miserable sinners," which prompts Hannay to glance at a nearby newspaper with an article about his case. The wife notices this, follows his gaze, reads the headline, and becomes worried. Hannay sees this and mouths reassurance. At this point, the praying husband opens his eyes and sees the two exchanging messages. Misinterpreting this visual evidence, he assumes that Hannay is what Hannay had earlier convinced the milkman he was. This situation is pure

Hitchcock: It presents his kind of characters and interactions, and it uses editing to show what people see and thereby reveal their thoughts and misinterpretations. The crofter, who pretends to be loving and righteous, and his wife, who pretends to be contented, could easily have been part of another, very different type of movie—the type that Hitchcock used to make. This sequence is the most insightful, sensitive, and real in the entire film. Its view of domesticity is loaded with implications about sex, religion, greed, jealousy, and frustration.

Professor Jordan provides a different view of domestic life's contradictions. Hannay arrives at Jordan's house during a birthday party for his daughter. Almost immediately Mrs. Jordan introduces him to "Patricia," an awkward young woman wearing glasses who evokes Miss Imery in *Rich and Strange*. Later, Jordan kisses his wife and this same young woman goodbye, which strongly suggests that Hitchcock once intended the character to be the professor's daughter. (Patricia is also the name of Hitchcock's own much younger daughter.) However, during a separate scene at the party a different woman, "Hillary," is specifically identified as the professor's daughter. This contradiction may have resulted from Hitchcock having second thoughts about what seems meant as a kind of practical joke on his own Patricia.

After the guests leave, the kindly host reveals he is the head spy. What makes this moment so rewardingly Hitchcockian is the fact that Jordan's menacing side is not isolated from his family life. As Jordan confronts Hannay, his wife (Helen Haye, who played Mrs. Hillcrist in *The Skin Game*) enters to announce that lunch is ready. Soon after, while Jordan holds Hannay at gunpoint, she again enters and mentions lunch, without revealing any surprise. These villains—a responsible husband and father, and his supportive wife—contrast revealingly with the barren marriage of the dysfunctional "good" couple, the crofter and his wife.

Hannay and Pamela are neither married nor in love; they are not even mutually supportive. At their first meeting on the train, he tries to elude the police by pretending they are lovers, but she betrays him which sets the tone for their later antagonism. On the run and bickering, they are as "handcuffed" together as the crofter and his wife, or any other mismatched couple linked by law and ceremony. The dialogue acknowledges this parallel as they set out: She asks, "What chance have you got tied to me?" and he replies, "Keep that question for your husband." When Hannay tells Pamela the truth about his predicament, she doesn't believe it, but she cooperates when he says he has killed women and his great uncle "murdered three wives." He describes himself as a "most sensitive child" who would "wake up in the middle of the night, screaming, thinking the police were after me...." (Does this derive from Hitchcock's own memory of childhood?) Although Fred and Em and the Lawrences are married, their bickering suggests that they are only "posing" as couples, just as Hannay and Pamela argue while pretending to be man and wife.

They stop at an inn where only a room with one bed is available. Without luggage, they register as a married couple and the innkeeper's wife assumes they are romantic runaways pretending to be married. She thinks she can see how very much "in love with each other" they are, whereas when alone they do nothing but argue. Still, their pose is closer to the truth than they themselves realize: They soon will fall in love and we have already noticed him gently adjusting her hairpin while she slept.

Once the film links Hannay with Pamela, his chase-quest overlaps with their evolving relationship. The latter is resolved

first, and it is appropriate that only after Pamela gets free of the handcuffs does she learn the truth about Hannay's innocence, which prompts her to stay with him voluntarily and leads to mutual understanding and trust instead of poses. Such true companionship is

Pamela and Hannay—a mutually antagonistic couple in *The 39 Steps* (Photofest)

visualized in the final close shot of the two holding hands, as the no-longer-relevant handcuff dangles empty from Hannay's wrist.

Pamela's recognition of the truth about Hannay resolves the film's personal issue, so from that moment on the spy-murder plot hurries to its climax at the theater, which, like the concert hall scene in *The Man Who Knew Too Much*, involves killing someone in a public space, the ultimate reality encountered in a place of entertainment and illusion. After shooting Mr. Memory to prevent him from answering Hannay's question about "the 39 steps," Professor Jordan tries to escape by leaping onto the stage and is cornered as the curtains close, and the show ends in a way that evokes Fane's equally public death in *Murder!*

The scene also reminds us again of Hitchcock's debt to the German silent film, and particularly Fritz Lang's *Spione*, in which one man dies while performing on stage and another survives because a bullet is stopped by an object in his breast pocket. In addition, the spies in *Spione* and also in Lang's *Dr. Mabuse* films

STARRING
Madeleine **CARROLL**
Peter **LORRE**
John **GIELGUD**
Robert **YOUNG**

From the play by Campbell Dixon
Based on the novel "ASHENDEN" *by*
W. SOMERSET MAUGHAM

DIRECTED BY
ALFRED HITCHCOCK   A 🅶🅱 PRODUCTION

are masters of disguise, and in that way they anticipate Professor Jordan, who is described in Hitchcock's *The 39 Steps* as a "brilliant agent" who "has a dozen names" and "can look like a hundred people."

Richard Hannay may have the ground pulled out from under him by outside forces, but he adapts well and keeps his balance. He does not make serious mistakes or suffer from self-doubt, which helped *The 39 Steps* become a popular entertainment—so popular that Hitchcock could follow it with two of his least commercially minded thrillers, *Secret Agent* and *Sabotage* (both released in 1936).

For much of its length, *Secret Agent* does not even try to blend a thriller, in which events dominate, with a drama of character and feeling. Instead, it treats the two separately, at times succeeding as a drama but often failing as a thriller. In one extended segment, however, it does create a dramatic and courageous blend of the two.

The novice spy in *Secret Agent* is the exact opposite of Richard Hannay: He chooses to become involved, he makes a serious mistake, and he suffers from self-doubt. Also, unlike Hannay and Pamela, this film's couple are significantly altered by their experiences, through which they learn about themselves and about life.

Like *The Man Who Knew Too Much* (but not *The 39 Steps*), *Secret Agent* has a moral issue at its center. In fact, the two films share the same moral issue. *The Man Who Knew Too Much* was set during peacetime and the Lawrences are told it is their duty as citizens to reveal what they know, although that will endanger their daughter's life. "Why should we care if some foreign statesman we've never even heard of were assassinated?" they ask. In reply, they are reminded of Archduke Ferdinand's assassination in Sarajevo: "In a month's time, because a man you've never heard of killed another man you've never heard of in a place you've never heard of, this country was at war." Ultimately, the Lawrences avoid making a decision about this by hunting for the villains themselves.

Secret Agent takes place during World War I, as Edgar Brodie, a novelist, is renamed Richard Ashenden and asked to commit himself to the larger good by joining the Secret Service. During this scene, Hitchcock graphically contrasts one person's limited significance with large-scale issues that affect thousands of lives: The camera shows a newspaper report of Brodie's supposed death, then pulls back to juxtapose it with the much bigger headline, "War in the East Nears Crisis." Ashenden accepts his duty readily enough, perhaps because it seems to require no personal cost beyond inconvenience. It is only after getting involved that he and the film's heroine encounter their moral struggle, one based on a far less hypothetical situation than what the Lawrences faced.

Hitchcock conveys this through a plot extracted from *Ashenden: The British Agent*, a 1927 collection of linked stories by W. Somerset Maugham, and from a play by Campbell Dixon based on those stories. Because the main character is an author by profession, Maugham's stories frequently contrast reality and melodrama, as Ashenden compares the fictional interactions he has created with his manipulation of real people. On one occasion, when a character brandishes a revolver, the daily-life "surroundings made the melodramatic scene in which Ashenden was engaged perfectly grotesque. His own play seemed to him much more real." Hitchcock probably felt drawn to this situation in which a creative artist, like himself, confronts the reality of the espionage he has depicted.

Secret Agent's screenplay combines elements from two separate plots developed in five of Maugham's stories. In "The Hairless Mexican," "The Dark Woman," and "The Greek," Ashenden and a professional killer, the Hairless Mexican (also known as the General), are sent to stop a Greek from delivering documents to the German embassy in Rome. Ultimately, the Mexican kills the wrong man, for the Greek had never even sailed.

"Gustav" and "The Traitor" deal with Grantley Caypor, an Englishman who is a German spy in Lucerne. Ashenden finds Caypor "gross and vulgar" and his German wife unpleasant, but he notes, "You could not but feel sympathy for a man who took so much delight in simple things," and he detects "a deep and sincere love" between the Caypors. Indeed, Caypor's wife (like Em and Hitchcock's other ideal women) "loved him, notwithstanding his weakness." When Caypor travels to England, Ashenden informs

In *Secret Agent* (1936), the Hairless Mexican (Peter Lorre)—and murder— come between Elsa (Madeleine Carroll) and Ashenden (John Gielgud). (Photofest)

his superior. Soon, Mrs. Caypor stops receiving letters and Ashenden assumes that her husband was arrested and executed. Mrs. Caypor continues to worry until one day their pet dog "sat down on his haunches and threw back his head and gave a long, long melancholy howl. Mrs. Caypor looked at him with terror.... The doubt, the gnawing doubt that had tortured her during those dreadful days of suspense, was a doubt no longer."

In adapting these stories, Hitchcock and his writers combined characters from one plot with events from the other. The result has Ashenden mistakenly believe Caypor is the enemy spy, so Caypor becomes the wrong man who is killed. *Secret Agent* also discards Caypor's negative characteristics, making him reliable, gentle, and friendly—qualities underscored by Hitchcock's casting of Percy Marmont, who had earlier embodied the sensitive, sensible male in *Rich and Strange*. In addition, Hitchcock shifted much of the

Madeleine Carroll, Peter Lorre, Hitchcock and Robert Young relax on the set of *Secret Agent.*

action to Switzerland, where the plot of *The Man Who Knew Too Much* had begun and where Hitchcock had spent his honeymoon.

To this material is added a Hitchcock-style romance by having Ashenden (John Gielgud) "issued" a "wife," Elsa Carrington

(Madeleine Carroll), as part of his pose. Thus, *Secret Agent* echoes *The 39 Steps*'s premise of two strangers pretending to be married who become a true couple because of and despite the harrowing events they share. Another new character is Robert Marvin (Robert Young), a handsome, charming American who pretends to pursue Elsa and turns out to be the actual German spy. Seemingly frank and impulsive, but entirely deceitful, Marvin contrasts with the Hairless Mexican who (in Peter Lorre's one-of-a-kind performance) is a murderer and sexual predator, but is also entirely honest, with an energetic spontaneity that can only be called a love of life.

Ashenden approaches his job with cool gentility until he becomes conscience-stricken at being involved in an innocent man's death. After that he grows more intense, but even then he only temporarily resists carrying out his distasteful duty. Elsa reveals more extreme changes and hence becomes the more overtly interesting character.

When Elsa meets Ashenden for the first time, her explanation of why she has become involved reveals her unappealing naïveté and self-centered shallowness. In fact, she sounds like someone who has seen too many films. "I've come to Switzerland for a thrill," she says, adding, "excitement, big risks, danger, perhaps even a little—" (she pretends to fire a pistol). Later, when she realizes that Caypor is the man to be killed, Elsa blurts out, "How thrilling!" Soon, Ashenden and the Mexican manipulate Caypor into hiking with them the next day and Elsa enthuses, "Wasn't it marvelous, the way he fell for it?" Ashenden responds, "I'm glad *you* enjoyed it, anyway." He takes no pleasure in what he is doing, which makes him less adolescent, but also rather dour and a bit tedious. "We're not hunting a fox," he lectures her. "We're hunting a man—a man with a wife. Oh, I know it's war and it's our job to do it, but that doesn't prevent it being murder, does it? Simple murder. And all you can see in it is fun." (This dialogue illustrates *Secret Agent*'s tendency to state—and overstate—judgments and viewpoints that Hitchcock's films usually imply.)

Caypor (Percy Marmont) has no idea what awaits him as he hikes with the Mexican and Ashenden in *Secret Agent*.

These scenes lead to the film's highlight, and an extensive, impressive one it is. Suspense is not involved here, for Hitchcock does not offer Caypor any way to escape his fate. Instead, the viewer is in the uncomfortable position of watching the steps that lead to Caypor's inevitable death—a position shared with Ashenden and Elsa. What Caypor would perceive as minor, everyday actions stand out to us because we know they will be among his last. For instance, in a cable car, as they start up the mountain, Caypor plays with a child, which is poignant rather than casual because of the context.

The three men's trek is intercut with Elsa (soon joined by Marvin) at the hotel taking a German lesson from Mrs. Caypor, with the worried actions of Caypor's dog opening or closing these scenes. Meanwhile, on the mountain, the reluctant Ashenden tries to stop events, then stays behind as the Mexican goes on with Caypor. After this, Ashenden watches through a telescope, helpless but (like the viewer) able to *see* the situation in detail. The intercutting of these three locations is more excruciating than tense as it leads to Caypor's "accidental" fall. With powerful subtlety, Hitchcock does not show the man being pushed, only the empty place where he had been, as we hear the dog's agonized howl on the soundtrack.

This sequence generates emotional force even though we assume, with Ashenden and his colleagues, that Caypor is an enemy agent and "deserves" to die. It takes on much greater power retroactively, after we learn that Caypor real-ly was the dignified and sensitive—and innocent—man he appeared to be.

The film's highlight has now ended, but the next few scenes still satisfy, if less completely. Attending a local festival, Ashenden and Elsa feel far from festive even before a telegram reveals that Caypor was the wrong man. As a performer spins a coin in a bowl, the sound grates on Elsa's nerves. Soon, Hitchcock evokes her state of mind by superimposing the button that had incriminated Caypor over the spinning coin. Then, he shows a multiple image of the button, as the Mexican is heard laughing at the absurdity of their mistake. Hitchcock admirably sought to visualize Elsa's distress, but the spinning coin is not a successful image of her state of mind; it is too odd and arbitrary.

Later, on a boat with Ashenden, Elsa is distraught and again the dialogue is more explicit than usual in a Hitchcock film. She says that now she knows what Ashenden is "real-ly like." She had fallen in love with him "at first sight," but that is over now. "Somehow I don't like murder at close quarters as much as I expected—or murderers, for that matter." She turns away from Ashenden, and the scene ends with an ambiguous shot of the lake's surface, perhaps intended to evoke both calmness and an unplumbed depth. At any rate, Elsa—like Em, in *Rich and Strange*—finds herself personally adrift while on the water.

Shortly after, Ashenden reveals that he was not present when Caypor was killed, and Elsa's love returns. The two agree to quit their jobs, then kiss and evidently consummate their "marriage,"

Ashenden and the Mexican hide in the dramatically lit bell tower of a Swiss church in *Secret Agent*.

for the next morning finds them giggling together as he declares, "It is almost a pleasure to be alive," and refers to their marriage as "the genuine article, today." It is as if the death of Caypor has brought them together by awakening a heightened sense of life.

Despite the general high quality of these scenes, *Secret Agent* feels as though Hitchcock had hurried into production before the script was finished. This is suggested by the film's tendency to verbalize ideas, instead of letting the viewers draw conclusions themselves. At one point, Ashenden tells the Mexican, "Fighting in the front line's a darn sight cleaner job than this," which leads the trio to discuss the situation further.

Plot manipulation undermines two of the film's set-piece scenes. In one, at a church in a picturesque village, Ashenden and the Mexican find that their contact, the organist, has been strangled at his keyboard. This situation strains to achieve its effect because the men take far too long to realize that the single prolonged chord they hear is not caused by the organist practicing.

After Ashenden and Elsa decide to resign, more plot manipulation occurs. The Mexican leads Ashenden to a totally new character, a young woman with whom he has spent the night and whose fiancé works in a factory that makes chocolate bars. Secret messages are received there and, on the day before, an important one arrived, which the fiancé will reveal in exchange for enough money for them to marry. This information, introduced abruptly thanks to the Mexican's off-screen activity, soon draws Ashenden away from Elsa and their mutual resignation.

As Ashenden and the Mexican tour the chocolate factory, someone on the production line writes a note and sticks it blatantly out of a box, which is sent along the conveyor belt. Noticing this, the Mexican follows the box until he sees a man's hands take the note, which warns that two English spies have arrived and tells the recipient to call the police anonymously. The man does so, although the first person could easily have called the police himself and his method of communication seems far from practical. When the police arrive, Ashenden sets off a fire alarm, which causes the workers to crowd out, thus delaying the police. Ashenden and the Mexican then try to elude a pursuer, who turns out to be the very man they came to meet. All of this activity feels both unconvincing and unnecessary, like a half-hearted imitation of a Hitchcock sequence.

After some further plot maneuvers, the film places its characters on a train to Greece. This final sequence is prolonged and anticlimactic, although the situation does effectively embody abstract meaning: As the train crosses the frontier into "enemy territory," it parallels the innocents' journey across a more abstract frontier of awareness and knowledge. In addition, it brings to a climax the moral dilemma established at the film's start.

Unfortunately, this sequence also includes excessive dialogue and unclear actions. Elsa holds a gun on Ashenden, refusing to let him kill Marvin or be involved in killing him. Ashenden declares

**Madeleine Carroll acts menacing in this posed publicity shot for *Secret Agent*.
(Photofest)**

that the choice is between Marvin's life and the lives of thousands
of soldiers. Elsa responds, "What do I care about them? What do
I care about him, even? It's us! We're not going to have this on
our conscience." Then, with his characters in this challenging

(if overly verbal) predicament, Hitchcock and his writers do not make them resolve it. Instead, an outside factor—an arbitrary, far-too-convenient train crash—interrupts the stand-off. Amid the wreckage, Ashenden starts to strangle the pinned and injured Marvin, then withdraws his hands. Next, in a series of unconvincing actions, the Mexican sits down near Marvin and foolishly places his pistol next to Marvin's hand; when Marvin asks for water, the Mexican removes a flask from his pocket while Marvin takes the pistol, shoots the Mexican, then collapses.

Two additional versions of these events are described in the book, *Hitchcock's Notebooks*. One is similar to the scene ultimately used, but the other is the clearest and most cynical of the three. In it the Mexican gives Marvin the flask and shoots him as he drinks from it, while Ashenden and Elsa look on "in horror." Then the Mexican, "alarmed at the possible loss of his brandy," grabs the flask from the floor, where Marvin has dropped it. He offers it to Ashenden and Elsa, who "turn away, shudderingly," and the scene fades out as the Mexican, "with a show of nonchalance," drinks the brandy himself.[3]

Ultimately, it is not clear if the film agrees with Elsa or with Ashenden or with neither. It does, however, suggest that Elsa is a creature of undesirable extremes, who exchanges her initial enthusiasm for a kind of guilty moralism, both of which seem inherently selfish. At any rate, the viewer is left with the impression that one cannot do what must be done in wartime without becoming soiled. In *Secret Agent*, Hitchcock conveys the complex, unsavory nature of being involved with the world, without denying the need for such involvement. Commitment results in contamination; life, honor, innocence, and truth are the price that must be paid by Hitchcock's dirty, guilty heroes.

In *Rich and Strange*, Fred had wanted "to experience life." More accurately, he just thought he did, because when it happens he cannot handle what he encounters. Here, Elsa and, to a lesser extent, Ashenden go through the same process. Their postcard note to the spy chief that ends the film sums up the results of experience

The Hairless Mexican, a "lady killer," with one of his conquests (Lilli Palmer) in *Secret Agent.*

for Fred and Em as much as it does for Ashenden and Elsa: "Home safely but never again."

Despite its emphasis on complex emotions and serious events, *Secret Agent* shares with *The 39 Steps* the use of witty wordplay that draws attention to the ambiguities of communication and mutual understanding. When Ashenden first encounters his assassin assistant, the Mexican is chasing a young woman. "Lady killer, eh?" Ashenden asks his boss. "Not only ladies," he is told. Later, as Elsa applies her make-up, she asks Ashenden what he thinks of his "new" wife. He replies, "I don't know. I'll tell you when you've finished putting on your face." Marvin, asked if he understands German, answers, "Not a word, but I speak it fluently." It falls, however, to the Mexican to voice what might be the basic Hitchcock question: "Maybe perhaps this lie is true?"

Verloc (Oscar Homolka), the home-loving anarchist, and his wife (Sylvia Sidney) in *Sabotage*. (Photofest)

In his next film, *Sabotage*, Hitchcock shifted back to an officially married couple, and this time he had a much more tightly constructed script. Still pushing the limits of what is permitted in a thriller, he pared away even more of the entertaining elements that had made *The 39 Steps* a hit. He denies his characters the verbal wit found even in the otherwise grim *Secret Agent*, settling instead for one short scene of physical comedy involving a boy's awkwardness in a kitchen. Overall, *Sabotage* is arguably Hitchcock's most consistently realistic sound film, one that rigorously avoids compromising its characters and story line.

In *Secret Agent*, Elsa became more central than Hitchcock may have intended or expected; in *Sabotage*, the wife naturally evolves into the main figure. At the same time, Hitchcock has shifted from a film about a reluctant hero to one with no hero at all, and to one without even an element of mystery, for Hitchcock reveals at the outset that the husband is an enemy saboteur (although his wife learns this only later). Nor is the setting colorful or exotic, but rather a section of working-class London. At the time, Hitchcock noted the danger this posed:

> I have tried lately to get interiors with a real lower-middle-class atmosphere — for instance, the Verloc's [*sic*] living-room in *Sabotage* — but there's always a certain risk in giving your audience humdrum truth.[4]

American title of *Sabotage*

Compared with *Secret Agent*'s awkward jumble of plot elements, *Sabotage* has very little story, concentrating instead on characters and their relationships. Hitchcock's source was a 1907 novel by Joseph Conrad, *The Secret Agent* (the title of which he had given to his prior film). As Hitchcock supervised changes and the addition of details, the process — as would happen with any creative filmmaker — brought the source material ever closer to himself. Hitchcock certainly identified with the working-class London milieu, familiar from his childhood, to which he added a greengrocer's shop that recalls his father's.

A portrait of stable family life: Mrs. Verloc, Stevie (Desmond Tester) and Verloc in *Sabotage*.

Another personal element relates to the husband, a seemingly average man who leads a secret life as an anarchist and a saboteur. In Hitchcock's hands, Verloc became not a melodramatic cliché but a self-portrait in metaphorical terms. Conrad described Verloc as an overweight man who instinctively "embraced indolence" and treasured "his repose and his security." Verloc "felt the latent unfriendliness of all out-of-doors with a force approaching to positive bodily anguish." Because his job "in revolutionary politics" was "to observe," he tended to be passive and cautious. Hitchcock surely must have identified with such a description.

In domestic terms, Hitchcock may also have felt a kinship to this story's seemingly stable married couple who are raising Stevie, the wife's much younger brother, as if he were their own child. The novel's Winnie Verloc married her husband for the security and protection he could provide for Stevie (who is mentally slow, an element omitted from the film) and herself. In return, she creates

Sylvia Sidney as Mrs. Verloc in *Sabotage*. (Photofest)

for Verloc a comfortable domestic environment. Appropriately, her mother had been Verloc's landlady, and the two women now serve very similar functions. Romantic love is not a factor here, but mutual support is. Verloc is comfortable with his wife and with the child he cares for, but he never feels truly close to either.

Certainly, Hitchcock did identify with Verloc's professional situation. In the novel, Verloc runs a small book shop where he also sells pornography, and Conrad refers to him as a man who lives "on the vices, the follies, or the baser fears of mankind." This "seller of shady wares" conducts his sabotage behind the scenes. When Hitchcock updated (and personalized) the novel, he turned Verloc into the manager of a movie theater, thus equating films with the original's "shady wares." The family lives in rooms located directly behind the theater's screen. Thus, reality can be found beneath the deceptive surface of projected illusions: A meeting of saboteurs is juxtaposed with an audience's laughter during a comedy, and a family dinner takes place while screams are heard in the theater.

Like the director himself, Verloc (Oscar Homolka) is a heavy-set man who works in the movie business. He seeks to lead a life that, on the surface, is quiet and without turmoil. His wife (Sylvia Sidney) describes him as "the quietest, kindest, most home-loving person," and he himself says, "Anything for quiet. I don't like attention being drawn to us...." Even after the police reveal an interest in Verloc, his wife calls him "the most harmless person in the whole world." As Hitchcock wrote about himself in 1956, "For a thriller-movie-making ogre, I'm hopelessly plebeian and placid."[5]

However, beneath his own "plebeian and placid" surface, Verloc is an anarchist who earns money by periodically throwing a scare into the public and disrupting their complacency. (The definition of "sabotage" given after the opening credits includes the aim of "alarming a group of persons or inspiring public uneasiness.") At the film's start, Verloc causes a citywide power blackout. "I hope you're satisfied with last night's show," he tells his employer, sounding like the movie exhibitor he is. "It wasn't as easy as it looked.... The sort of thing to make people sit up. I think you'll agree I've earned my money."

A link is implied in *Sabotage* between acts that frighten the public harmlessly and the theoretically harmless violence in the films Verloc shows—and Hitchcock makes. Both Verloc and Hitchcock plan and execute plots intended to disrupt and disturb the public. Hitchcock wrote in 1936, shortly before making *Sabotage*:

> I am out to give the public good, healthy, mental shake-ups. Civilization has become so screening and sheltering that we cannot experience sufficient thrills at first hand. Therefore, to

prevent our becoming sluggish and jellified, we have to experience them artificially, and the screen is the best medium for this.[6]

Such a remark is especially curious coming from a man who could himself be called "sluggish and jellified," at least physically.

Hitchcock must also have been aware of the way the film reflected his other harmless anarchistic tendencies. For example, after tea breaks on the set, he enjoyed tossing the teacups over his shoulder. "I can't explain it," he told a reporter in 1937, "but breaking things makes me feel fine."[7]

Verloc draws the line at anything that has a permanent impact on people, at doing something that could cause loss of life. He is, however, ordered to plant a bomb in the cloak room of the subway station at Piccadilly Circus, where innocent people will probably be killed or injured when it explodes. He will not be paid unless he does this job and, it is implied, he has come to rely on this income. So he compromises his principles and sets to work.

Unfortunately, the police are suspicious and keep close watch on Verloc. Thus prevented from making the delivery himself, he sends Stevie to put the package in a locker at the station. Along with the package, he has Stevie carry a film, *Bartholomew the Strangler*, and warns him not to take it on public vehicles because nitrate film stock is explosive. By linking the bomb with a movie melodrama, Hitchcock inevitably inspires thoughts about whether such films are harmless or destructive.

At this point, Hitchcock begins a sequence that takes the intensity of Caypor's murder in *Secret Agent* several steps further. Having established that the bomb will explode at a certain time, he calmly shows Stevie distracted by a series of events, from a toothpaste demonstration to the Lord Mayor's Parade. Everything is presented straightforwardly, without elaborate intercutting, for only the viewers and Verloc know what excessive delay will mean and only the viewers know that Stevie *is* being delayed. Eventually, the boy ignores Verloc's warning about film's explosive nature and boards a bus, sitting next to a woman and her little dog. Now Hitchcock intercuts among Stevie, the package, and various clocks until the appointed moment arrives.

Stevie's journey is nine minutes of precise, careful filmmaking that take the viewer on as excruciating a journey as Hitchcock ever provided. We know what might happen and are forced to watch despite our increasing dread, until the explosion destroys the bus and all its passengers. (In a sense, it is Verloc's profession—motion pictures—that destroys a family member and other innocents, as well as a pet dog.) The impact of this sequence derives entirely from Hitchcock, not Conrad, for in the novel the person blown up is initially assumed to be Verloc, because of a coat label, and only gradually do the characters and the reader realize that it is Stevie.

This is not the first time Hitchcock has dramatized the possible loss of a child, but Stevie's death may have deeper roots in the director's psychology. According to the documentary, *Hitchcock, Selznick and the End of Hollywood,*[8] Hitchcock as a child enjoyed traveling on the local streetcar. "One Sunday," states the narrator, "he miscalculated and found himself unable to get home. When he finally arrived, hours later, he found his father waiting for him at the door." This transgression, we are told, prompted the father to send the boy to a police station where he was locked in a cell. If true, this incident lends a vividly personal overtone to the sequence in which the innocent Stevie pays the ultimate penalty merely, it seems, for riding on a bus. Indeed, in Hitchcock's mind the incident could have created a basic aversion to travel by linking it with severe punishment. (Some skepticism is called for here, because

A posed publicity portrait of the triangle in *Sabotage*: the anarchist, the policeman (John Loder) and the anarchist's wife. (Photofest)

neither of Hitchcock's biographers could cite a reason for the jail cell punishment and it is not clear what source the documentary's author, Michael Epstein, had for his statements.)

Until Stevie's death, *Sabotage* has emphasized Verloc and his dilemma, although some attention is given to Ted (John Loder), a Scotland Yard detective who, disguised as a neighboring greengrocer's assistant, watches Verloc's movements. Hoping to gain information, he takes Mrs. Verloc and Stevie to lunch at Simpson's, an upscale restaurant. Later, we deduce Ted's growing personal interest in Mrs. Verloc when he tears up a petty cash refund voucher; he realizes that the lunch became more a personal matter than a business expense. Because of this conflict between duty and private inclination, Ted asks to be taken off the case, but, he explains, "In my job you have to do as you're told." Verloc could make the same statement. (John Loder may be charmless as Ted, but he is rather believable in a role that does not require charm. A more smoothly appealing actor, like Robert Donat, would have disrupted the film's otherwise consistent sense of reality—despite Hitchcock's later claim that he had wanted Donat for the role.)

The film shifts its emphasis to Mrs. Verloc when she learns about Stevie's death, leading to a superb sequence that exemplifies Hitchcock's belief that "things... are as important as actors" and "can richly illustrate character."[9]

As her husband confesses everything to her and declares, quite convincingly, that he did not mean any harm to come to the boy, his movement by chance leads her attention (and the camera's) to Stevie's model boat, in a fine example of using a nondescript object to evoke thoughts and feelings. Verloc blames Ted, whose interference kept him from delivering the bomb himself. Then, Verloc's tactless comment, "If we had a kid of our own," prompts his wife to walk out. In the theater, she stops and, despite everything, a Walt Disney cartoon makes her laugh. But the cartoon is "Who Killed Cock Robin?" and when the bird dies she snaps back to reality.

In one of Hitchcock's most subtle tour-de-force scenes, Mrs. Verloc enters the dining room and starts to serve dinner. Looking down, she notices that she is using a knife. She pauses, then thrusts her utensils away and picks up more harmless ones. She glances at the unused place setting and empty chair where Stevie would have been, then continues serving only to realize that the knife is again in her hand—she must have picked it up unconsciously, in response to her thoughts of Stevie. Struggling between a compulsion to punish Verloc and a conscious refusal to kill, once more she puts aside the knife, more abruptly this time. At this point, Verloc notices her hand flitting near the knife and fears the worst. He rises and moves around the table into a tight close-up that crowds the viewer's vision. Standing opposite each other, only inches apart, the husband and wife pause, then both reach for the knife—he to prevent her from using it on him and she in a combination of instinctive attack and instinctive defense. She grabs it first, and he grunts. The knife has entered his stomach, as if with a will of its own, and Verloc collapses to the floor.

All of these psychological details are conveyed through a careful selection and ordering of close and medium shots that reveal to the viewer far more than the characters themselves realize about what is occurring. And these details are all Hitchcock's contribution; in the novel, Mrs. Verloc's stabbing of her husband is much more deliberate. This sequence is an ideal illustration of "pure" cinema, and in 1937 Hitchcock cited it as an example of his desire to use editing "to draw the audience right inside the situation instead of leaving them to watch it from the outside, from a distance."[10]

Verloc has been depicted with unexpected sympathy for a saboteur: He doesn't want to hurt people; Stevie's death is not deliberate; and, like Professor Jordan in *The 39 Steps,* he is a stable provider for his wife and "child." Ted, in contrast, is a surprisingly unsympathetic representative of law and order: He is pushy, arrogant, awkward, and devious. Both men often lie to or mislead or manipulate Mrs. Verloc. When she kills her husband, she does so with justification, without planning, and almost without awareness of the act. Like Alice White in *Blackmail*, she then tries to confess and her policeman boyfriend compromises his duty by covering up for her.

At the end, fate protects Mrs. Verloc when a bomb carried by her husband's associate destroys the house and her husband's body, leaving her free from suspicion. Nonetheless, a viewer must wonder if the guilt she and Ted share (the kind of guilt that Elsa, in *Secret Agent*, sought to avoid for herself and Ashenden) will be a burden that gradually corrupts their relationship. Moral ambiguity pervades *Sabotage*, making it psychologically and emotionally, as well as cinematically, a high point of Hitchcock's art.

Sabotage is thoroughly grim in its dissection of this working-class domestic structure, this seemingly stable family in which the husband and wife share a marriage of convenience and the child is not really theirs. The husband may cause the child's death and the wife may kill the husband, but both seem helpless in the grip of chance and their own limitations. The events in *Sabotage* form a tragedy almost Greek in its nature, except that the characters lack stature.

Disguised as a greengrocer's assistant, Ted (John Loder) flirts with Mrs. Verloc in *Sabotage*. (Photofest)

"When I set out to put the fear of death into people," Verloc's employer tells him sternly, "it is not helpful to make them laugh." He could be speaking here for Hitchcock and about *Sabotage*. In *The Man Who Knew Too Much* and *The 39 Steps*, a death occurred near the film's start and its main function was just to set the plot in motion, so both films were permitted an extensive use of humor. But in *Secret Agent* and *Sabotage*, a death occurs well into the story, the victim is known to the audience, and the event has dramatic impact, so Hitchcock includes much less humor.

Hitchcock in these two films stretches the allowed limits of a popular genre by killing off innocent characters. In later years, he voiced regret at this, calling the way he handled Stevie's death "a grave error on my part" and "a serious mistake."[11] Verloc might have been speaking for Hitchcock when, after the blackout interrupts a film showing, he agrees to refund the patrons' money,

Ted confronts the Verlocs with his suspicions in *Sabotage*.

explaining to his wife that it "doesn't pay to antagonize the public."
Because neither *Secret Agent* nor *Sabotage* was a box-office hit,
when Hitchcock regrets such scenes we hear the voice of the
businessman and the entertainer, while the artist remains silent on
the sidelines. In a drama, it would be permitted for an innocent
character to die in such a way and for a director to dramatize that
death, but the conventions of a thriller would not permit it. As
Hitchcock wrote in 1937, "The art of directing for the commercial
market is to know just how far you can go."[12] Here, he discovered
the answer—but he would, of course, keep testing those limits.

After *Secret Agent* and *Sabotage*, Hitchcock acknowledged
his need for wide popularity. While planning *Young and Innocent*
(1937), he wrote of appeasing the public's "natural craving for
romance, drama, and comedy."[13]   In another article, published

during the same month, he stated, "We are controlled by popular appeal. It is no use for a director to make a success artistically if the company loses money on the picture."[14] Then, after completing *Young and Innocent*, he mentioned that film's high cost of production, adding, "When you are working with those figures there does not seem much hope of experimenting with new ideas." He concluded that efforts to appeal to everyone have caused filmmakers

> ...to come down to the common simple story with the happy ending.... The cost of making a picture is so great... that we find it difficult to get our money back, even for a successful film with a universal appeal, let alone in films that have experimented with the story or the artist. That is the thing

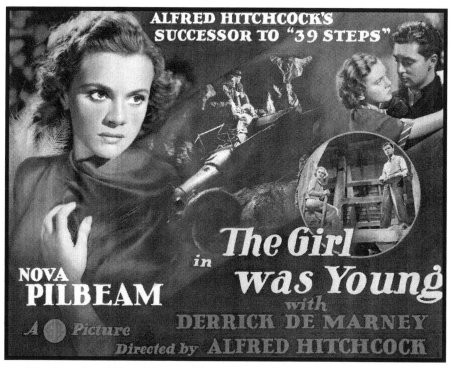

The American title of *Young and Innocent* (1936) was *The Girl Was Young*.

that has kept the cinema back. I should
say it has pretty well gone a long way
to destroy it as an art.[15]

In *Secret Agent* and especially *Sabotage*, the characters do not achieve stability; indeed, we are left with the impression that they have been tainted by events. Considering those films' grim intensity, even if they had been financial successes Hitchcock probably would have sought a change of pace. In *Young and Innocent* he returned to the more optimistic tone found in *The Man Who Knew Too Much* and *The 39 Steps*, a decision that also helped re-establish his reputation as an entertainer. Thus, he revived the situation of an innocent man on the run, only this version is more relaxed than the fast-paced *The 39 Steps* and its implications are more wholesome; the word "innocent" in the title has two meanings—the hero is innocent of the murder of which he is accused, and the hero and heroine are youthful innocents maturing into adulthood. Like its title, this film perfectly illustrates Hitchcock's ability to combine a crime melodrama and a "traditional" drama into a single seamless narrative, a kind of double exposure.

Hitchcock's previous three films were all adapted from respected works by long-established authors, but next he turned to Josephine Tey's *A Shilling for Candles*, a rather ordinary detective novel published in 1936. It was only Tey's second mystery, the first having appeared (under her real name, Elizabeth MacKintosh) a full seven years before. As a whole, this novel is precisely the kind that Hitchcock never found interesting: It features a murder investigation conducted by a Scotland Yard Inspector who sifts clues, questions suspects, uncovers motives, and checks alibis. Occasionally, its attention shifts to a newspaper reporter following the case, but the only character who springs to vivid life is Erica Burgoyne, a self-reliant girl of 17 who is the local chief constable's daughter.

Erica enters the book when Robert Tisdall, a young man suspected of murdering a woman, faints and she tends to him, using her Girl Guide knowledge. The main evidence against him

In *Young and Innocent,* **Tisdall (Derrick de Marney) and Erica (Nova Pilbeam) are pursued by her father, the chief constable. (Photofest)**

is a coat button found tangled in the woman's hair, and Tisdall claims his coat was stolen several days earlier. After he flees to avoid arrest, the book spends three chapters (of its 27) following Erica. She accidentally meets Tisdall and, believing him innocent, brings him some food, then sets out to find the person who took his coat. At a diner she meets a truck driver who on the day in question had given a lift to a traveling china mender, so she tracks that man down and learns that he did take the coat, but later sold it. Before the day is over, though, Erica has Tisdall's garment, complete with all of its buttons, which she presents to the inspector. This removes Tisdall from suspicion, but the fugitive does not know that and remains hidden (and out of the plot) until near the book's end. As for the inspector, he sorts out the other suspects and eventually arrests the guilty party.

Aside from appearing in her three chapters, Erica pops into the action a few times, but that is all, so it is interesting to watch Hitchcock's mind at work here. He and his writers discard almost

Erica and Old Will (Edward Rigby) seek the real murderer in *Young and Innocent*. (Photofest)

everything related to the official investigation and build the film around Erica and Tisdall. In the process, although the book does not link her with Tisdall romantically, the film has her join him in his flight and his search for the coat, turning the couple into a younger, more innocent version of Pamela and Hannay from *The 39 Steps*. Another major change discards the inspector and replaces him with Erica's father, the chief constable (who barely exists in the novel). Thus, Erica not only aids a fugitive but also goes against her father in doing so. The closest the book comes to such a conflict is when Erica is described as "growing up" because she might have to lie to her father about where she has been; this brief reference becomes the essence of the film.

The similarity to *The 39 Steps* and the possibility of making a lighter film surely appealed to Hitchcock, but another factor is also at work. Hitchcock evidently had enjoyed working with Nova Pilbeam, who played the daughter in *The Man Who Knew Too Much*, and she was now exactly Erica's age, so he must immediately have pictured her as the character. This, in turn, leads us to consider Hitchcock's presentation of children in his films to date.

Prior to 1934, the parent-child relationships in Hitchcock's films almost always involved adult children who depend on, or are influenced by, one or both parents. These films feature the child as the main character, with the parents functioning as background figures (*The Lodger* and *Blackmail*) or manipulators (*Easy Virtue* and *Champagne*). It is probable that Hitchcock identified with such children.

Alfred Hitchcock's own daughter, Patricia, was born on July 7, 1928, and this evidently modified her father's frame of reference. It can hardly be a coincidence that his first official cameo role, the first in which he sought to be noticed, was in 1929 (*Blackmail*) and it presented Hitchcock as a subway passenger tormented by an undisciplined child. *Rich and Strange*, in 1932, emphasized Fred and Em as a couple, but at the end Fred considers having a child — as if their relationship were steady enough for them to raise a family (it hardly seems to be), or perhaps he thinks a child will bring them closer.

As if in response to this thought, *The Man Who Knew Too Much* two years later features an equally unstable couple who have a young daughter. The feeling about children suggested by the *Blackmail* cameo returns here, as the parents joke about disowning their child, but they ultimately discover a sense of responsibility and a concern for her welfare. A threat to the daughter forces them to mature, forming a closer bond between themselves and with the child. Significantly, this child is a young one, not an adult, and the film's emphasis is on the challenged and overwhelmed parents. Had Hitchcock — at least temporarily — ceased identifying with intimidated children? The married couple in *Sabotage* is also raising a young child who is in danger, only this time the father is not truly the father and the threat comes not from outside the family but from within, from the father's inability to separate his work from his domestic life.

Hitchcock and his writers build *Young and Innocent* around a girl and her relationship with her father (Percy Marmont), and in a sense this girl is the same one as in *The Man Who Knew Too Much*, the now slightly older surrogate for Hitchcock's daughter. The father in *The Man Who Knew Too Much* feared losing Betty in an extreme, melodramatic way, and Colonel Burgoyne has a similar fear when he learns Erica is with a possible murderer (Derrick de Marney). However, Hitchcock has adroitly built into the plot and the relationships a second layer that functions on a natural, more universal level. To do so, he altered, and sometimes reversed, the content and implications of Tey's novel. Thus, almost everything interesting about *Young and Innocent* was not in the original source.

Here, again, Hitchcock uses his plot as a melodramatic metaphor that embodies the characters' more universal feelings and needs. Thus, the crime investigation and escape-chase story line—a policeman fears for a girl in the hands of a possible murderer—is bound together with the story of a young girl discovering romance, of her growing up and breaking away from family and childhood and innocence, of her becoming progressively more estranged from her father, and of the parent's resistance to that change. This is the kind of situation any father could encounter, even if he isn't a chief constable and the intruder isn't an escaped prisoner.

Indeed, similar situations already appeared in some of Hitchcock's previous films. For example, the mother in *Easy Virtue* resists losing her son to an intruder. She therefore perceives Larita as a threat and is certain she conceals "some vile secret" from them. This attitude is shared by Daisy's parents in *The Lodger*, by Kate's father and Philip's mother-surrogate in *The Manxman*, and by Mrs. Hillcrist in *The Skin Game*, who exposes Hornblower's daughter-in-law as a disruptive influence on his household. In *Champagne*, a father tries to prevent his daughter from marrying her boyfriend and, by extension, seeks to keep her dependent on him. In a similar way, Joe in *The Lodger* becomes jealous of the unknown male to whom the girl is attracted and suspects he represents a more obvious kind of danger.

In *Young and Innocent*, Erica finds herself drawn away from family, father, and childhood by a charming, mysterious outsider.

Erica and Tisdall are a youthful fugitive couple in *Young and Innocent*. (Photofest)

Her father, naturally wary, perceives the potential boyfriend as a threat to her (and, unconsciously, to his own relationship with her), turning the story into a father-daughter-boyfriend triangle. From his perspective, this intruder is dangerous, because he threatens to disrupt the previously stable domestic arrangement, one in which Erica also functions as a mother-substitute for her siblings. To her father, it becomes an either-or situation: him or me?

The film depicts the search for the missing coat in a series of episodes that take Erica progressively further away from her immediate family and toward recognizing her attraction to Tisdall. She starts by bringing him food. Then, when interrupted by two policemen, they flee together in her car. At this point, she is disturbed at running away from one of the officers, but not just because he represents the law. He also is a link with growing up, with an aspect of her old life that prepared her for this moment:

"He taught me how to drive," she tells Tisdall, as she and the young man drive away. This is the first major indication that Erica is becoming assertive and independent, going out on her own and taking chances. Thus, the police are linked with Erica's youth and with the family structure—the authority from which she must break free to set off on an unpredictable life, even though it feels like a betrayal of the support and guidance she had earlier received.

With Erica at the wheel, they stop at an intersection. The branch on the right leads back to town (home, security, the past), the other to the diner where Tisdall had lost his coat (the unknown, a new life, the future). Because of road repairs, the right fork is blocked, so they are forced to go left, although Erica says she would have picked that route, anyhow. After they drive on, we see the barrier being removed, as if fate or chance had timed events to limit her options. This is an explicit case of Hitchcock giving literal, visual form to an internal, emotional situation, as Erica must choose between going back to her father or forward to that which is unfamiliar and possibly dangerous.

Now that Erica has committed herself, they visit the diner and learn that the china mender is probably staying at a tramps' lodging house. First, though, to explain her trip Erica stops at her aunt and uncle's house, arriving during their daughter's birthday party. Tisdall stays by the car, but the uncle notices him and says, "I can't leave you out here like a criminal." The fact that Erica did not remember the birthday, although previously she never missed a year and always brought a present, further dramatizes the shift in her outlook and interests.

The aunt suspects "something's going on between them" and tries to keep the couple from leaving, but the sympathetic uncle (like the innkeeper's wife in *The 39 Steps*) sees them as a romantic couple and helps them escape. The uncle may be wrong about the facts, but he is right about their innocence. However, the intrusive aunt telephones the girl's father, saying, "I feel it's my duty to tell you" about the visit. She warns him, "Erica's so young. She's at an awkward age."

Erica, Tisdall and Old Will hide in the abandoned mine in *Young and Innocent*.

The father is surprised and disappointed, because she has always told him where she was going and with whom. He then calls ahead and has a policeman stop her car, but, when the officer does, he recognizes Tisdall and again they flee. This becomes a turning point for Erica. "I can't go back now," she says, in dialogue that would easily fit a non-thriller context. "Poor father, what shall I tell him?"

That night, she sleeps in the car while Tisdall locates the china mender, who has the coat, but someone else had given it to him with the belt already missing. (In the film, the belt is the crucial item, not a button as in the novel, perhaps because a button had already been a misleading clue in *Secret Agent*.) Again pursued, the three hide in an old mine, but the flooring collapses and the car with Erica in it hangs precariously over a pit. Up to this point, the developing relationship between Erica and Tisdall has been revealed in small ways; for example, when she says, "Oh, Robert, I hope things turn out all right," he reacts to her calling him "Robert" and responds, "They're starting to." Now, as Erica no longer has solid ground beneath her, she and Tisdall reach for each other until they grasp hands and he pulls her to safety. This is a suspenseful, if familiar, rescue situation, but it also neatly embodies their developing relationship, as she puts her trust in him and he keeps her from plunging into an abyss.

After this emotional peak, their relationship suffers a set-back when Erica is caught and returned home, where her scrupulous father imposes guilt on his errant daughter by taking the responsibility upon himself and writing a letter of resignation. Both Erica and her father, in equally sympathetic depictions, are torn between personal feelings and social responsibility (as were Frank in *Blackmail* and Ted in *Sabotage*, although in somewhat different contexts).

That night, Tisdall escalates his challenge to paternal rule. Before, Erica had met him out in the world, but now he invades domestic security by secretly entering not just her house but her bedroom. She greets him with an embrace and declares, "I did it because I wanted to." Their mutual commitment has now been achieved and acknowledged, so the mystery aspect of the plot must also reach a conclusion: They find a clue in Tisdall's coat pocket, which leads smoothly and swiftly to the murderer's capture. Then, with her suitor's reputation restored, Erica asks her father, "Don't

you think we ought to ask Mr. Tisdall to dinner?" Through Erica's efforts, the father begins to accept change not as a threat but as something natural and positive. He shakes hands with Tisdall, as the film ends on a close-up of Erica looking back and forth at the two men in her life, uniting them with her smile.

Although *Young and Innocent* has a positive (but not sentimental) view of courtship, it does include a few gratuitous criticisms of marriage, which is consistent with Hitchcock's other works. *The 39 Steps* had contained

168

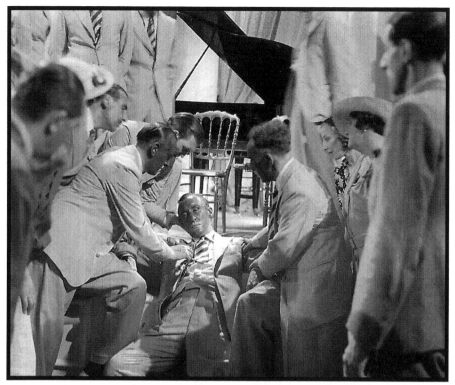

In *Young and Innocent* the real murderer is accidentally discovered playing in a dance band.

many such references, usually in the form of comic relief, whereas *Secret Agent* offered only one, but a starkly un-comic one: Early in the story, Elsa reacts to a criticism by slapping Ashenden, who immediately slaps her back: "Married life *has* begun," she declares. In *Sabotage*, when a policeman offers to perform a dangerous task because the other man has a wife, the second man responds that that is all the more reason why he should do it himself.

To this list, *Young and Innocent* adds two couples—less young and far less innocent—who certainly provide negative role models for Erica and Tisdall. The film opens with a bitter argument, which leads to murder, between a woman who got a Reno divorce and her jealous husband who refuses to accept it. Later, in the court case that precedes Tisdall's, a married couple decides not to get a separation order. When the judge orders the husband to "keep the peace for six months," the wife asks if he couldn't make it eight months, to take her through Christmas. As the two leave, they have already begun arguing. (Is arguing, to Hitchcock, a major part of a typical marriage?) Relevant, too, is the fact—retained from the novel—that Erica's relaxed and responsible father has no marriage partner.

Also consistent with Hitchcock's obsessions is this film's frequent, often witty references to vision, usually faulty, and to events or words that are misperceived or inspire ambiguity. The future murderer, in the opening scene, insists on his own version of events, and his distinguishing characteristic—a squint—is related to his eyes, to his vision. Tisdall, after discovering the body, turns and runs, which produces two conflicting interpretations: Was he running away or running to get help? Later, he tells the police he had sold a story to the victim, so an officer writes down that he "received money from her on former occasions," which is technically accurate but entirely misleading.

In *The Man Who Knew Too Much*, Nova Pilbeam's character had made a more accurate judgment of Ramon than her father did, and here she also "sees" clearly and accurately. After Tisdall collapses in the police station, an officer says that he "passed out—or pretended to." Erica replies, "Of course he's passed out. I'd have told that a mile off." When she comments, "He doesn't look like a criminal," the officer cautions her, "Don't let looks influence you, young lady." To this she replies, with innocent confidence, "I don't" (a response that Hitchcock underlines by using a close-up).

Erica's clear vision is contrasted with the limitations of many adults. Tisdall's obtuse defense attorney is so dependent on his glasses that losing them renders him helpless. Then the police bring the wrong man into court and, hunting for their prisoner, they don't notice him sitting in plain sight. As with the judge in *Easy Virtue*, these representatives of the legal system literally have faulty vision. (Outside, Hitchcock himself, holding a camera, is frustrated at not getting a clear view of events.) In another fine, understated example, Erica, Tisdall, and her supportive uncle elude her blindfolded and uncomprehending aunt during a game at the birthday party.

Young and Innocent may contain no tour-de-force editing sequence (like Verloc's death in *Sabotage*), but it does make expressive use of film technique. In one scene, Erica has lunch with her father and siblings, and when the others discuss Tisdall's plight, Hitchcock shows only Erica as she—and we—hear comments that build sympathy in her for the fugitive. (This is the same technique Hitchcock used in *Blackmail*'s more famous "knife" sequence, only without taking the extra step of distorting the sound.) Later, after Erica is caught and brought home, she has dinner with the other children, but this time her father's empty chair in the foreground draws attention to his absence.

With *Young and Innocent*, Hitchcock re-established his ability to entertain, not antagonize, audiences, but he did so using his own mixture of tension, wit, and subtle, multi-leveled intelligence. This may have been a deliberate move, for he had a reason to shake the image of a "serious" filmmaker: In the late spring of 1937, he asked his agent to negotiate a Hollywood film contract for him.[16] To a man as wary of travel and the unfamiliar as Hitchcock, this would be a major step, and it also would be a major professional risk to leave his secure position in Britain for an uncertain future in the United States. But Hitchcock was so determined to venture forth that he even rejected offers by American companies, like M-G-M, to direct for them in England.

With all of this in his mind as he prepared *Young and Innocent*, Hitchcock must have responded to the fact that in *A Shilling for Candles* the murder victim is a British popular entertainer who moved to Hollywood and became a success. Clearly, moving to Hollywood can have negative side effects! *Young and Innocent* expands on this by making Tisdall an English film writer who, in Hollywood, had sold Christine a story and was left money in her will, which became a possible motive for murder. Thus, his seeming success in Los Angeles returned to haunt him! It is probably no coincidence that author Charles Bennett, who had collaborated on all of Hitchcock's films since 1934, had recently left for Hollywood.

After shooting *Young and Innocent*, Hitchcock decided to stir up interest in himself by visiting America, so he, Alma, and Pat sailed to New York City in late August 1937. They returned to London in September and Hitchcock, without a new project in the works, took the unusual step of accepting an already-completed screenplay, by Frank Launder and Sidney Gilliat, who had quite faithfully adapted *The Wheel Spins*, a 1936 novel by Ethel Lina White.

The novel, upon which *The Lady Vanishes* would be based, tells of Iris, a "vain, selfish, and useless" young woman who never takes other people into consideration. On the last day of her vacation in an unnamed European country, Iris briefly becomes lost in the mountains. "Thrown on her own resources, she had not the least idea of her direction," and her inability to speak any language but English increased her feeling of helplessness.

The next day, at the railroad station, Iris unexpectedly collapses from what is later diagnosed as sunstroke. Regaining consciousness, she suffers from exaggerated perceptions and senses "a general and secret hostility" toward her. Once on the train, she is befriended by Miss Froy, an Englishwoman employed locally as a governess. Already vulnerable, Iris is further disoriented when she awakens from a nap to find Miss Froy gone, and the other passengers deny that she ever existed. Some English travelers could support Iris's claim, but they refuse to become involved for various personal reasons, so Iris receives a taste of her own self-centeredness. At the same time, this woman, who has been interested only in bright young people like herself, now becomes "involved with the fate of an obscure and unattractive spinster."

As Iris seeks to prove that Miss Froy exists and to find her, events further undermine her confidence in herself and others. At one point, a fake Miss Froy appears, and a doctor in a neighboring compartment (accompanied by a bandaged patient and a nursing-sister) recommends that she visit a hospital. As the action evolves, Iris is drawn to Hare, a young engineer who helps her and to whom she notes, "Miss Froy is bringing us together, isn't she?" Iris also realizes the emptiness of her friends and her prior life. "There's

The LADY VANISHES

not one real person among the lot of us," she admits, and adds, "I'm wasting my youth."

Iris is encouraged when steam on a window reveals where Miss Froy had written her name on the glass, but soon the doctor arranges to give her a drug—which backfires and makes her confident, so she removes the patient's bandages and reveals Miss Froy. It turns out that Iris had blundered into a conspiracy—planned by the doctor—to eliminate Miss Froy, who unknowingly could implicate her politically powerful employer in a murder.

It is easy to see why Hitchcock responded to this novel's story line, for it contains many of his own interests, such as helplessness and distorted perception. It even features a character who—like so many Hitchcock figures—is shocked by "reality" into maturity, self-awareness, and responsibility, a process paralleled by a developing interdependence between her and a man.

Some of the novel's other characters could also have been written with Hitchcock in mind, such as the Todhunters, a supposedly married couple who in fact are illicit lovers. "Mrs." Todhunter, discontented with her husband, saw in this "rising barrister" a

Gilbert (Michael Redgrave), evicted from his own room, invades that of Iris (Margaret Lockwood), in *The Lady Vanishes*. (Photofest)

chance to improve her status. But Todhunter is even more self-absorbed and deceitful, for he has no intention of divorcing his wife, who has "both a title and wealth." By now, "Mrs." Todhunter has learned that "while he was careless of his own failings, his standard for women was so fastidious that she found it a strain to live up to it" (a statement that Em could easily have made about Fred, in *Rich and Strange*).

To these characteristics, the film adds the fact that Todhunter has a chance to become a judge and doesn't want to risk his reputation with a scandal. "You must think of it from my point of view," he tells his mistress (sounding like Philip Christian, in *The Manxman*). Then the woman, more to trap him into a scandal that will cause a divorce than to help Iris, admits that she saw Miss Froy; later, Todhunter tells his mistress that she might end up divorced, but his wife would never divorce him, so she changes her mind and identifies the fake Froy to save her own reputation.

Another topic that would have appealed to Hitchcock is the emotional effect of travel—the feeling of helplessness in a foreign country and the resulting fondness for one's secure home. Miss Froy, in the novel, likes to travel mainly because she appreciates "the joy of the return." Other characters attempt to bring home along with them; as one notes, "If we didn't dress [for dinner], we should feel we were letting England down." However, love of country has its limits. When Iris appeals for Hare's support because he is English, he replies, "You mustn't confuse patriotism with prejudice."

Related to travel is the challenge of communication, and even knowing another language does not fully solve that problem. In the novel, Hare contrasts a language professor's knowledge of grammar with his own ability to "swear in the vernacular." On the other side, a local waiter learned English at school and can "rattle off strings of English phrases. But the first time he heard the language spoken by a Briton, he was unable to understand it."

According to Donald Spoto, Hitchcock made only a few changes to the Launder-Gilliat script, so most of the differences between the film, *The Lady Vanishes* (1938), and the novel probably do not derive from him (although he certainly accepted them). However, he reportedly did supervise some changes in the opening and closing sections, and added a sequence in the train's baggage car.

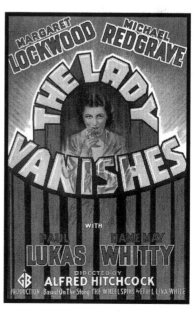

One major change replaces Iris's adventure on the mountain with a prolonged introduction to the characters at their hotel the night before departure. Here Iris (Margaret Lockwood) reveals her boredom with life. "I've no regrets," she tells her two friends. "I've been everywhere and done everything.... What is there left for me but—marriage?" Here, she sounds like Alice White in *Blackmail*, but she also sounds a bit like a Hornblower (from *The Skin Game*) when she mentions her plan to marry for money and status: "Father's simply aching to have a coat of arms on the jam label." This engagement and its implications about Iris were not in the novel, and although the film introduces them here, they are not referred to again until much later, which suggests that Hitchcock did not have time to integrate them fully.

Also introduced are Caldicott and Charters (Basil Radford and Naunton Wayne), two new characters who are distressed by loss of contact with home. They refer to "England on the brink" and make comments like "If only we knew what was happening in England" and "Our communication's cut off in a time of crisis," but it turns out they are only concerned with a cricket test match. They are wrapped up in their own nationality and ignorant about other countries; they once mistook the "Hungarian Rhapsody" for Hungary's national anthem, but at least they were respectful enough to stand during it.

In the film, the sympathetic engineer, Hare, becomes Gilbert (Michael Redgrave), who is researching a book on folk dance. On the last night at the hotel, he has some locals demonstrate a dance in his room and the noise disturbs both Iris and Miss Froy (Dame May Whitty). As Miss Froy remarks to Iris, "Some people have so little consideration for others. It makes life so much more difficult than it need be, don't you think?" Thus, the film's heroine and hero both lack consideration for others (although Gilbert at least has the excuse of his work), and during the story their initial antagonism evolves into mutual trust and responsibility.

A key alteration involves broadening the story's canvas. What in the book functioned only on a personal and local level becomes more political and international in the film. At one point in the novel, Hare offered a deliberately far-fetched explanation of events: "Miss Froy," he theorized, "is a spy who's got some information which she's sneaking out of the country." The film

The Todhunters (Linden Travers and Cecil Parker) confront Caldicott (Naunton Wayne) in *The Lady Vanishes*. (Photofest)

adopts this wild, inaccurate guess as the actual explanation, with Miss Froy shifting from a woman unknowingly involved in a local problem to one who knowingly carries "the vital clause of a secret pact between two European countries" coded in a piece of music. As a result, Iris does not suffer from sunstroke, but is hit on the head by a flowerpot dropped from a window and seemingly intended for Miss Froy.

As an outgrowth of this change, the other characters are no longer just people who avoid getting involved in strangers' problems. Now, they represent ways of responding to confrontations between countries, and these political overtones dominate the film after the conspiracy and the threat have been exposed.

At first, Charters and Caldicott try to avoid trouble. "Thing like this might cause a war," says Charters, adding that it is "up to us to apologize and put the matter right." When he steps into

Dr. Hartz (Paul Lukas) and the nursing sister who wears high heels (Catherine Lacy) in *The Lady Vanishes*.

the doorway to do so, he is promptly shot in the hand. Up to this point, the two have anticipated the policy of appeasement that the British would soon adopt toward Germany, but once they do take the situation seriously, they commit themselves to fighting with courage and competence.

Todhunter, too, insists that confrontation be avoided because "it would mean an international situation," but his response is based more on fear than politeness. When the shooting starts, he refuses to fight and although he possesses a pistol he will not use it or let the others use it. "I don't believe in fighting," he declares, to which Caldicott replies, "Pacifist, eh? Early Christians tried it and got thrown to the lions." Ultimately, Todhunter seeks to save himself by approaching the enemy waving a white handkerchief and he is immediately killed—the fate of the passive and cowardly when confronting ruthlessness.

The ultimate point is stated outright by the politically committed, gently courageous Miss Froy: "One must take risks." Beyond that, though, *The Lady Vanishes* offers no subtle or complex commentary on war and confrontation. This simplistic advocacy of commitment is not what one expects from the mind and feelings of Hitchcock. Even this close to the start of World War II, he would probably have offered a view closer to that in *Secret Agent*: Political commitment may be necessary, but it also involves inevitable contamination. In this regard, *The Lady Vanishes* probably owes more to Launder and Gilliat than its director.

Also atypical of Hitchcock is the film's limited emphasis on the heroine's psychological distress, which the novel develops fully, with frequent reference to Iris's vision and perceptions. For example, the author states that Iris "saw sections of faces floating in the air" and "was conscious of... lights flashing before her eyes"; the other passengers "appeared as bleared and distorted as creations in a nightmare." Iris felt "as though she were in a dream, where every emotion is intensified," then came "near the borderline of that world which was filled with shifting shadows — where fantasy usurped reality." Finally, "To her distorted imagination, the faces of these strangers were caricatures of humanity — blank, insensible and heartless."

True, Hitchcock does offer a few distorted subjective shots. When Iris watches her friends waving good-bye as the train pulls away, he puts the image out of focus, and when she starts to faint, he uses a series of multiple images (as he had done in his silent films). Much later, viewers share Iris's perception in shots that superimpose Miss Froy's face over the other passengers. Such moments are effective — as were similar ones in *Secret Agent* and *Sabotage* — but it is surprising how few of them Hitchcock included in a story built around the heroine's mental state.

In fact, the film in general lacks Hitchcock's distinctive use of visual style and implication to communicate information and emotion. Certainly, the scene in which the seemingly sympathetic Dr. Hartz (Paul Lukas) offers Iris and Gilbert drugged brandy is

"Mrs." Todhunter with Caldicott and Charters (Basil Radford) during the shoot-out in *The Lady Vanishes*. (Photofest)

vintage Hitchcock, with the two glasses large in the foreground, dominating the characters, but far more common are scenes featuring extensive conversations, presented in what Hitchcock himself might have disdained as "photographs of people talking." In one case, a single two-shot of Iris and Gilbert runs uninterrupted for more than a minute.

Happily, the conversation is lively and entertaining (if extensive), the people are likable or at least interesting (if unsurprising), and the plot is involving (if not entirely clear, either at the time or retroactively). Even the extraneous seven-minute sequence in the baggage car, which adds nothing to the plot, is enjoyable in its mixture of humor and serious violence as Gilbert and Iris struggle with a fellow passenger. Overall, the film fully established Hitchcock's ability to entertain audiences in a more mainstream mode than he generally found congenial. Whether that

Charters, Iris and "Mrs." Todhunter during the final shoot-out in _The Lady Vanishes_. (Photofest)

result derived from chance circumstances or from calculation by the director, _The Lady Vanishes_ served as an ideal calling card to the Hollywood studios, a testament to the fact that Hitchcock was not as "arty" or "foreign" as some of his recent films suggested.

With _The Lady Vanishes_ finished and with Hollywood still very much on his mind, Hitchcock and Alma, but not Pat, left London in June 1938, and again sailed for New York. This time, they moved on to Los Angeles, where in July negotiations were completed and he signed a contract with producer David O. Selznick. Then he returned home. Because his commitment to Selznick would not begin until April 1939, Hitch-cock had time to make _Jamaica Inn_, a romantic thriller set in the early 1800s and based on Daphne du

Maurier's popular 1936 novel. Hitchcock agreed to make this film for Mayflower Pictures, a company run by producer Erich Pommer and actor Charles Laughton, with Laughton to star.

Even before shooting started, Hitchcock seemed uncomfortable with the project, referring to it as "the Laughton vehicle." He added, "Usually I do not like historical subjects...."[17] In later years, Hitchcock did all he could to distance himself from the film. "When I saw what this was going to be," he said in 1963, "I tried to get out, but I'd already taken money from them so I couldn't."[18] His disinterest was probably due at least partly to the distraction of planning to leave for America.

One problem, as Hitchcock pointed out in a 1939 lecture at New York's Columbia University, was that toward the end of the book the local clergyman is revealed as the chief villain, after which he dominates the story. An important actor (i.e., Laughton) would have to play this character, Hitchcock explained, but the casting of such an actor would telegraph to viewers that the character is not as innocuous as he at first seems. Therefore, Hitchcock chose to reveal the character's involvement quite early, which adds tension by letting the audience know more than certain characters do. He also changed the character from a clergyman to the local squire, perhaps to avoid offending religious-minded viewers.

The novel tells its story from the innocent heroine's perspective, revealing information only as she learns about her uncle Joss's criminal activity. At first she believes it is simple smuggling. Then, she realizes that Joss and his gang wreck ships and murder anyone who attempts to reach shore. The film also leaves Mary (Maureen O'Hara) in the dark, but it reveals key information to the viewer, handing the story to Joss (Leslie Banks) and Squire Pengallan (Laughton) by giving them scenes of which Mary is unaware.

Although in many ways this is not a typical Hitchcock film, it does include elements that echo his earlier characters and concerns. One aspect that probably stirred his interest is the relationship between Joss and his wife, Patience. The novel describes Patience

Squire Pengallan and Jem Trehearne (Robert Newton) in *Jamaica Inn*. (Photofest)

as like "a whimpering dog that has been trained by constant cruelty to implicit obedience." Even Mary, who likes her aunt, refers to the woman's "pathetic dumb stupidity." In the film, Patience's commitment to Joss becomes more like that of Em to Fred in *Rich and Strange* and of Mrs. Verloc to her husband in *Sabotage*. She says he is a good husband and she would change nothing about him, "even if I could." Much later, when Mary calls Joss "a wrecker" and "a murderer," Patience responds, "But he's my husband.... You don't understand. You don't *know* him." Soon after, she adds, "I love him. People can't help being what they are. Joss can't. I can't. There's nothing to be done." This kindly, gentle   victim of Joss's dominance will not leave him. In the   stormy climax, Patience is told (as in *The Man Who Knew Too Much* and *Secret Agent*) that the lives of many men are in balance against the life of one, Joss. "Yes," she replies, "but he's my man." At the same time, Joss's pomposity and bluster mask a childlike helplessness, a dependence on others that in a more malevolent way recalls Fred in *Rich and Strange*.

In another familiar plot element, Mary helps Jem (Robert Newton), a member of the gang, to escape when the gang thinks he has betrayed them. Hiding out in a cave by the sea, the two are antagonistic and start to bicker, much as Hannay and Pamela did in *The 39 Steps*.

Aside from the married couple, Joss and Patience, and the brief bickering of Jem and Mary, *Jamaica Inn* contains little that recalls the content or visual style of Hitchcock's other films. The editing fits the traditional American formula, in which a long shot is followed by closer views, not the more distinctive Hitchcock-Soviet style. The resulting film maintains a viewer's interest, but it does so in rather conventional ways.

Jamaica Inn is, however, unusual in the way it reflects Hitchcock's life and career. Consciously or unconsciously, the director turned the film's chief villain into a surrogate for himself and his own situation, so much so that his later protestations of

Jem and Mary (Maureen O'Hara), who briefly become *Jamaica Inn*'s fugitive couple. (Photofest)

disinterest in *Jamaica Inn* start to sound like a way of disguising this autobiographical self-revelation.

As embodied by Charles Laughton, Squire Pengallan is a sociable, overweight, superficially respectable man who hosts (and dominates) dinner parties and who savors good food and drink, while financing that life by planning and directing the commission of crimes. In his first scene—appropriately, at one of his dinner parties—Pengallan is self-satisfied and superficial. He enjoys playing host, but only as long as he is the center of attention. Pengallan is concerned with his creature comforts: with food, with port wine and brandy, with warming himself before "a good fire," and with beauty. "I know what to *do* with money, when

**A confrontation between the Squire and Jem as Mary looks on in _Jamaica Inn_.
(Photofest)**

I have it," he says. "That's why I _must_ have it." Unfortunately, as the squire's faithful servant reveals, several bills from the butcher and the baker remain unpaid.

One can easily picture this squire as a satiric portrait of Hitchcock in his social mode, but it is striking that Hitchcock himself painted this portrait. At the film's end, Pengallan's parallel to the director becomes even more clear-cut.

In the novel, after the clergyman is revealed as the criminal mastermind, he attempts to flee with Mary, but doesn't get off the moors. The film develops the squire's similar plan in greater detail. He intends to leave the country, but only after one final wreck, one last job (i.e., this last film). After the crime, the squire ties Mary up and forces her to accompany him, but when he insists that she wear a cloak, his sexual interest takes on an overtone of practicality (the

Joss Merlyn (Leslie Banks), the wrecker and murderer, and his boss, the Squire, in *Jamaica Inn*. (Photofest)

garment will cover her bonds) as well as one of paternal concern. "It's wise to wrap up well while this cold wind's blowing," he says to her, as to a child. Thus, Mary becomes for the squire both sexual partner and daughter.

From the carriage in which he abducts her, the squire points out his house. "I may never see it again," he tells her. "Because, you see, we may never be able to come back. We may be going a long way, you know. Nearer the sun, of course." The squire refers to Italy or Greece, but Los Angeles is also "nearer the sun" than England. "I always knew," Pengallan adds, "that to live like a gentleman, graciously and with elegance, I *must* have money — and a few beautiful possessions, of course, like you, my dear." Soon after, his servant tells a visitor that Pengallan has "gone away on business."

With Mary in a cabin on board ship, the squire explains that he never cared for wrecking, but it "had to be done. Half my friends living like paupers, but I'm living like a prince!" When their pursuers catch up with them, Mary sympathetically says that Pengallan "doesn't know what he's doing.... It's not his fault. He can't help himself." After she escapes from him, the squire climbs into the ship's rigging. Looking down at the crowd of observers below, he declares, with dramatic flair, "What are you waiting for—a spectacle? Well, you shall have it." Then, like the aerialist in *Murder!*, he leaps to his death.

Before starting work on *Jamaica Inn*, Hitchcock knew that he and his wife and his daughter would soon leave Britain for a different life in Hollywood. This was a chance for advancement, but he also was moving to a new country, a new work environment, a new world. That would be stressful for anyone, but for Hitchcock such uncertainty about his future, his career, and his reputation would have been especially daunting. Given these circumstances, it is revealing of Hitchcock's state of mind that in this film's climax (which differs from that of the book) the squire's situation clearly parallels Hitchcock's. Each man had maintained a stable and respectable life-style, while profiting financially by directing crimes and murders that he did not himself commit. Now, after a career of extensive achievement through careful planning, each seeks to leave England for a land "nearer the sun" and compels his wife-child to accompany him.

Others think Pengallan has gone mad—he even suspects so himself—and here we can detect Hitchcock's own uncertainty about his break from a successful past. Pengallan's attempt ends in failure, with an abrupt fall from the height to which he had climbed. Is Hitchcock's transporting his wife and child to a new world also a mad act? Is he committing professional suicide? By the end of *Jamaica Inn*, Pengallan has taken over the film, which ends not with a shot of the rescued Mary embraced by Jem, but with a close-up of Pengallan's servant, whose sorrowful expression reveals his

The Squire is trapped on board ship as he tries to escape with Mary in *Jamaica Inn.* **(Photofest)**

sympathy for the deluded squire, and Hitchcock's empathy for the misguided but daring actions of his surrogate.

As Hitchcock, with Alma and Pat, left England in the spring of 1939 for the sunny land of California, he no doubt hoped to remain the paternalistic manipulator he was at home by planning the execution of new crimes or leaving that way of life behind and making non-thrillers. In *Jamaica Inn*, despite the number of creative hands involved, Hitchcock left behind a typically honest and typically disguised record of the uncertainty that constantly hovered behind his public image of forceful confidence.

Realism and surrealism combine in *North by Northwest*. (Photofest)

CHAPTER EIGHT

REALITY AND THE IRRATIONAL

"I would like to make documentary films."
— Alfred Hitchcock[1]

"I practice absurdity quite religiously!"
— Alfred Hitchcock to François Truffaut, 1962

Alfred Hitchcock's basic plots about average people caught in unusual situations are not what set his films apart from those of his peers. What does distinguish them is the skillful way he blends mainstream themes into thriller plots, plus his ability to express meaning through "pure cinema." However, Hitchcock's films—especially his sound films—are further distinguished by the fact that within this voluminous individual existed two repressed and quite incompatible figures struggling to emerge: a documentarian and a surrealist.

Although attracted to the idea of documentary filming, Hitchcock did not want to shoot unrehearsed action—he called such directors "discoverers"[2]—because that would prevent him from controlling the images and, through them, a viewer's response. However, he was intrigued by projects that would bypass fictional plots and characters, while still allowing him full use of film technique. As he wrote in 1938:

> I would like to make documentary
> films, because here you have slabs
> of action or movement which can be

easily treated by photography and cutting.[3]

As early as 1927, he had enthused about "what a lovely film of rhythmic movement and light and shade we could make out of cloud studies." Such films, he noted enviously, "have been attempted on the Continent, where they frequently make pictures for love rather than profit."[4]

Probably influenced by the German silent feature, *Berlin—die Symphonie der Grossstadt* (*Berlin—The Symphony of a Great City*, 1926), Hitchcock wanted "since 1928" to film "what lies behind the face of a city—what makes it tick—in other words, backstage of a city" from dawn to dawn.[5]

He told François Truffaut:

> ...I can see the whole picture from beginning to end. It's full of incidents, full of backgrounds, a complete cyclic movement. It starts out at five A.M., at daybreak, with a fly crawling on the nose of a tramp lying in a doorway. Then, the early stirrings of life in the city. I'd like to try to do an anthology on food, showing its arrival in the city, its distribution, the selling, buying by people, the cooking, the various ways in which it's consumed. What happens to it in various hotels; how it's fixed up and absorbed. And, gradually, the end of the film would show the sewers, and the garbage being dumped out into the ocean. So there's a cycle, beginning with the gleaming fresh vegetables and ending with the mess that's poured into the sewers....You could take it through

the whole city, look at everything, film everything, and show all of that.[6]

In 1930, Hitchcock worked with playwright Sean O'Casey on an unfinished semi-documentary screenplay that, according to John Russell Taylor, used "the comings and goings in a small public park during one day as a sort of microcosm of city life."[7] Seven years later, replying to a hypothetical question about what he would make "if I were free to do exactly as I liked," he proposed "a verbatim [record] of a celebrated trial," a "fire at sea," and "a film of the Derby" presented as "a sort of pageant.... I would show everything that goes on all round the course, but without a story."[8] In 1938, this list expanded to include the General Strike of 1926, a mine disaster, and "an incident of sabotage in the Glasgow dockyards."[9]

Hitchcock's first Hollywood picture was intended to deal with the sinking of the *Titanic* and would have let him depict a cross-section of true, slice-of-life events. However, when faced with the opportunity, Hitchcock evidently wavered. In 1977, he told Donald Spoto that nothing about the project "struck me as very interesting,"[10] although just a year before he had described some of his ideas in detail. After establishing that the ship had struck an iceberg:

> ...I wanted to go to a card table, where four men were playing poker: go close to the whiskey and soda...the level is changing in the glass, tilting, you see?

At this point, the audience would think:

> "Here are the innocent people, they don't know what's going on." We might go down to the kitchen and I'd

see a chef is putting the final touches to a beautiful cake with a pastry bag.... And the audience would say, "Don't bother! Don't bother! It's never going to be eaten! The ship's going down!"[11]

Back in 1938, Hitchcock wrote that he wanted to make this film, but claimed that the "shipping companies are trying to prevent me" from doing so.[12] That may have been true, but he may also have had second thoughts about departing from his formula of presenting characters with a danger that might be overcome.

When he explained why his other ideas went unfilmed, Hitchcock offered similar rationalizations. In the case of the Derby film, he blamed the public. "Perhaps the average audience," he wrote, "isn't ready for that, yet."[13] Hitchcock also said that the British Board of Film Censors vetoed the General Strike idea. "Again and again, I have been prevented from putting on the screen authentic accounts of incidents in British life."[14] Nonetheless, the real problem may have been Hitchcock's by now automatic urge to disguise his serious subjects as superficial entertainment. The city film, therefore, "would have to be funny, and it would also require a romantic element.... It's an enormous task, yet I feel the need to do this picture."[15] The need remained and as late as 1973 he was still mentioning the project.[16]

In isolated sections of his films, Hitchcock depicted how things are done—the process of arrest and booking that opens *Blackmail*, for example—but he almost always resisted using this approach throughout an entire feature. After all, he declared disdainfully, "total plausibility and authenticity merely add up to a documentary."[17] Indeed, Hitchcock's documentary impulse was continually in conflict with an attraction to a very different style, one that negated all plausibility.

Hitchcock was drawn to surrealism in his private life as much as in his work. Often, his practical jokes were designed to create surreal situations for others, such as the 1930s dinner party he gave at which, with no explanation, all the food was blue. "I had the soup dyed blue, the trout, the peaches, the ice cream," Hitchcock recalled in 1965. It was the "best practical joke I ever played."[18] This example clearly links Hitchcock to the surrealist artist, Man Ray, who years later (in 1958 and again in 1971) created very realistic loaves of blue bread out of painted plaster.

Hitchcock depicted mental states in an extreme way, such as this shot from *The Lodger.*

Before *Rich and Strange*, Hitchcock had often depicted mental states in an extreme, phantasmagoric way. When he chose to limit such breaks with realism, his urge in that direction had to be satisfied by other means. Instead of modifying the look of his scenes, he made their events more fantastic and dreamlike, while the way he depicted them remained realistic. This brought Hitchcock close to the incongruity of surrealism, although he usually undercut the impact by offering logical explanations for the seemingly inexplicable.

According to Luis Buñuel, the best-known surrealist filmmaker, surrealism denied the function of logic and reason, of cause-and-effect and psychology. In his first film, *Un Chien Andalou (An Andalusian Dog*; France, 1929), Buñuel and his collaborator, the painter Salvador Dali, depicted events that have no logical relationship to each other, but are presented as if they do, with deadpan irrationality. Thus, characters can enter a scene or leave it without warning, and one situation or setting can evolve into another without explanation. During *Un Chien Andalou*, a person in an upstairs city apartment opens a door and steps directly onto a beach, as if that were the most natural thing in the world.

Such a dreamlike linking of concrete details is akin to the episodic, free-associational structure of *Number Seventeen*,

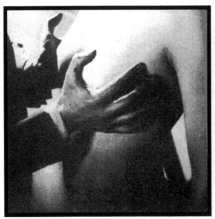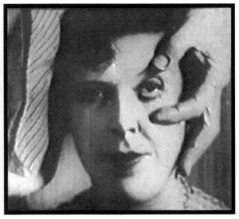

Dreamlike images from *Un Chien Andalou* (*An Andalusian Dog*, 1929).

The 39 Steps, and *North by Northwest* (1959). *The 39 Steps*, for instance, shifts from the main character being shot to him talking calmly with a sympathetic sheriff; before long, he is marching in a temperance parade, then giving a political speech. These juxtapositions, as Hitchcock said about *North by Northwest*, illustrate "the free abstract in moviemaking" and "the free use of fantasy, which is what I deal in."[19] *Un Chien Andalou*, however, both implies and negates rational relationships, whereas *The 39 Steps* and *North by Northwest* only *seem* to negate them, for their plots offer explanations. The appeal of the irrational is present, but in diluted form. Only in *The Birds* (1963) did Hitchcock allow himself to indulge fully "the free abstract in moviemaking" by including no explanation of the film's irrational events and surreal images.

The perfect Hitchcock-style surrealist painter was not Salvador Dali, who often depicted impossible objects and nonexistent landscapes, but René Magritte, who placed familiar, even ordinary, subjects in unnatural relationships. For example, one of Magritte's pictures depicts a bedroom filled from floor to ceiling with a giant apple. Some of Hitchcock's practical jokes are also based on such incongruity, as when he "used his maximum ingenuity to get gigantic pieces of furniture installed in friends' tiny flats while they were away."[20]

A dreamlike image from Hitchcock's *The Birds* (1936) which stars Tippi Hedren. (Photofest)

One also finds this quality in shots like those in *The Lady Vanishes* and *Notorious* (1946) of what appear to be large glasses or a coffee cup that dominate the humans who share the frame with them. Of course, such images are essentially "realistic" (the glasses and cup only seem large because they are supposedly closer to the camera than the people) and they have "meaning" (the drugs they contain justify the objects' inflated significance), but the visual impression they create is still surreal.

In *Marnie* (1964), Hitchcock sought a Magritte-like juxtaposition of incongruous elements in a single shot. "I wanted to show something that had always fascinated me—I think I'd seen it in Copenhagen and London, as well as in Baltimore, where *Marnie* takes place—a row of houses and suddenly a ship looming

In *Marnie* (1964), the mental state of the title character (Tippi Hedren) affects the look of the film. (Photofest)

above them," but with no water in view. Unfortunately, the shot's obvious special effects undermined the necessary realistic look.

"We were very pressed for time, or I would have scrapped the whole thing and started over."[21]

Although such shots evoke the director's feeling for poetic incongruity, they miss the surreal purity of moments like one in Buñuel's last film, *That Obscure Object of Desire* (Spain-France, 1977), a work that Hitchcock once said he liked.[22] In it, a man pauses on the street to admire the infant being held in a woman's arms; everything here is concrete, realistic, and mundane, except for the fact that cradled in the blanket is a pig, not a human baby.

Hitchcock's eccentric incongruity also appears in *Secret Agent*'s opening, which depicts the conclusion of a funeral. After the mourners leave, a one-armed man casually lights a cigarette, then grasps the closed coffin and wrestles clumsily with it until the box drops to the floor and is revealed to be empty. The film makes no attempt to explain the disorienting unpredictability of this man's actions and manner, which undermines the work's effectiveness as an espionage thriller while revealing the surrealist in Hitchcock briefly rejecting the need to offer a comprehensible narrative.

At times, Hitchcock's deliberate disruption of logic is more verbal than visual. In Maugham's *Ashenden*, a character explains why the assassin is known as the Hairless Mexican: "Because he's hairless and because he's a Mexican." This perfectly reasonable response clearly did not appeal to Hitchcock, for in *Secret Agent* we find a more surreal statement: "We call him the Hairless Mexican.... chiefly because he's got a lot of curly hair and isn't a Mexican." Similarly, in the novel *The 39 Steps* the title simply refers to a staircase, but in the film it quite pointedly does not.

Surreal moments appear more often in Hitchcock's British films than his later Hollywood works, because the director felt freer to indulge his imagination. As he explained:

> ...the audience would accept more...
> and one didn't have to worry too much
> about logic or truth. When I came to
> America, the first thing I had to learn
> was that the audiences were more

questioning. I'll put it another way. Less avant-garde. In the first *Man Who Knew Too Much*, the characters jump around from one place to another—you're in a chapel, and you've got old ladies with guns—and one didn't care.... If the idea appealed to one, however outrageous it was, do it! They wouldn't go for that in America.[23]

In *The Man Who Knew Too Much* a desperate fight takes place in a church sanctuary.

Hitchcock might also have mentioned, from *The Man Who Knew Too Much*, the image of two pistols resting on a church collection plate, or the sight of grown men hurling chairs at each other in a sanctuary where sun worshippers have been conducting a service at night! In *The Lady Vanishes*, the nursing-sister who wears high-heeled shoes offers an equally surreal incongruity.

Even in Hollywood, the surreal still attracted Hitchcock. In the 1950s, for instance, he agreed to film a novel, *The Wreck of the Mary Deare*, about a cargo ship found in the English Channel with just one man aboard. This situation reminded Hitchcock of the *Mary Celeste*, a ship "discovered, in full sail, in the Atlantic. People who boarded the ship found the lifeboats, the galley stove was still hot, and there were the remnants of a meal, but no sign of life." The appeal of such a "beautiful setup" is the fact that it is inexplicable—surreal—and Hitchcock realized that any explanation a writer might provide would inevitably be "terribly laborious" and "very trite,"[24] so he did not make the film.

The most acceptable way to include surrealism in a Hollywood film was to place it in the context of a dream, but to Hitchcock dreams and reality look alike. For *Spellbound* (1945), he wanted

One of the surreal images shot for use in the dream sequence of *Spellbound*. (Photofest)

"to break with the traditional way of handling dream sequences," which used "a blurred and hazy" image. Seeking "great visual sharpness and clarity," he convinced producer David O. Selznick to hire Salvador Dali as a designer.

> My idea was to shoot the Dali dream scenes in the open air so that the whole thing, photographed in real sunshine, would be terribly sharp. I was very keen on that idea, but the producers were concerned about the expense. So we shot the dream in the studios.[25]

Hitchcock had already thought along these lines in 1927, regarding *Downhill*. "I wanted to show that the young man was having hallucinations," he recalled.

Gregory Peck is the dreamer in *Spellbound*. (Photofest)

> In those days dreams were always
> dissolves and they were always
> blurred. Though it was difficult, I tried
> to embody the dream in the reality, in
> solid, unblurred images [and using]
> just straight cutting.[26]

A year later, in *Champagne*, Hitchcock did something similar by easing viewers unobtrusively into the heroine's fantasy of being attacked, and only afterward revealing that the events never happened. This technique resembles Buñuel's in *Belle de Jour* (France-Italy, 1967), except Buñuel did not clarify the distinction between dream and reality and Hitchcock did.

At times, Hitchcock's contradictory attractions to surrealism and the documentary converge. Always interested in how things

The beleaguered Manny (Henry Fonda) and his vulnerable wife, Rose (Vera Miles), in *The Wrong Man.* (Photofest)

work, Hitchcock-the-documentarian was impressed by automobile assembly lines and, in *North by Northwest*, he wanted to show the construction of a car "from a simple nut and bolt" to the moment when the vehicle is ready "to drive off the line." At this point, Hitchcock-the-surrealist would cause the impossible to happen: When the car's door is opened, a corpse falls out. Hitchcock-the-dramatist then sought to integrate this scene into the film's plot, but he couldn't find a way to involve the corpse in the overall story and so discarded the whole idea.[27]

The Hitchcock film that most thoroughly merges documentary reality and surreal atmosphere is the unjustly overlooked *The Wrong Man* (1957), which was based on real events. Hitchcock has stated that:

> For the sake of authenticity everything
> was minutely reconstructed with the

Manny and Rose seek proof that he is *The Wrong Man*. (Photofest)

people who were actually involved
in that drama. We even used some of
them in some of the episodes.... We
shot on the locations where the events
really took place.[28]

This posed publicity shot sums up the situation, for although Manny's wife is not accused, she suffers at last as much as he does in *The Wrong Man*. (Photofest)

The reconstructed real events in *The Wrong Man* are not, however, those of everyday life, for we watch as the main character is plucked from his doorstep by the police, driven to several locations in the city, then arrested and jailed. For this man, under these circumstances, even the smallest, most ordinary action or object has a dreamlike—or nightmare—quality: He moves, helpless and bewildered, through a world that seems to function with an unswerving but alien logic. The clarity of Hitchcock's shots and the precision of his editing only heighten the feeling of irrationality for the character and for the viewer. As Hitchcock says in his introduction to the film, this is "a true story" that feels "stranger than all the fiction" he had previously filmed.

Made 25 years after *Rich and Strange*, *The Wrong Man* is a remarkably courageous venture, one in which Hitchcock again explored content and form in fresh and challenging ways—

Innocent but imprisoned: the essential Hitchcock situation in *The Wrong Man*. (Photofest)

albeit without autobiographical overtones. And, as happened in 1932, critics and audiences could not accept the result. When discussing *The Wrong Man* with François Truffaut, Hitchcock reveals considerable interest in the film, until Truffaut starts telling him how he *should* have shot it, whereupon Hitchcock retreats, refusing to argue or debate. "I don't feel that strongly about it," he claims, and suggests that they file it "among the indifferent Hitchcocks." At least outwardly, he tried to agree with his critics and his public—"Let's just say it wasn't my kind of picture"—but in fact *The Wrong Man* truly *was* his kind of picture, one in which he allowed himself to deviate from the expectations he himself had cultivated.

Although *The Wrong Man* was not a popular success, Hitchcock's attraction to both documentary detail and surrealist incongruity continued to influence his films, adding an inimitable resonance to otherwise melodramatic action. The clash of these incompatible styles is typical of the way Hitchcock himself embodies opposite qualities. An orderly man, he made films about disorder; an entertainer, he depicted unpleasant events; a personal creator, he posed as a businessman; an experimenter, he assembled a commercial product. These contradictions help give Hitchcock's films the extra distinction that still sets them apart from those of his rivals and imitators.

Having learned to disguise his character studies as superficial entertainment, Hitchcock maintained that illusion by declaring that he had little interest in "content" and that his only concern was using film technique to control a viewer's emotions. Perhaps he came to believe these statements, after repeating them for decades, but most of the time his characters are not just an excuse to present the action. Instead, the action reflects and affects the characters. By training his public and the critics to believe the opposite, he was able to maintain a long and secure career, and within its self-imposed limitations he accomplished a great deal. Like the best dramatists, he blended character with action, often rendering the two inseparable. Like the best artists, he mixed conscious expression with unconscious revelation, often leaving viewers uncertain where the first ends and the second begins.

Nevertheless, Hitchcock became a prisoner—not of his genre, as he often claimed, but of his own defensiveness, a defensiveness that resulted from having revealed himself in *Rich and Strange* and then having that exposure rejected on all sides. Thereafter, he hid behind the not-uncomfortable mask of an entertainer, while continuing to explore his thoughts and feelings in the medium for which he had such a tremendous affinity.

Notes

Preface
1. *News Chronicle*
2. Hamden, Connecticut: Archon, 1977

Chapter One
1. Truffant, 21
2. Truffant, 19
3. Spoto, 68
4. *London Evening News*
5. Schickel, 301
6. Spoto, 84
7. Balcon, 26
8. Spoto, 89, 92
9. Spoto, 98
10. Taylor, 67
11. Spoto, 92
12. Ibid 101
13. Ibid 117
14. Martin, 127
15. Truffaut, 19

Chapter Two
1. Encyclopaedia Britannica, 1965
2. Truffaut, 17
3. Truffaut, 111
4. Taylor, 70

Chapter Three
1. *Who's Who in Filmland*, 1931
2. Spoto, 65
3. *McCall's*
4. Truffaut, 20
5. Spoto, 17
6. Spoto, 37
7. Spoto, 18
8. Spoto, 18

Chapter Four
1. Footnotes to the Film
2. Martin, 127
3. Footnotes to the Film
4. Martin, 127

Chapter Five
1. *Stage*, 1936
2. Footnotes to the Film
3. Bogdanovich, 12
4. Truffaut, 197
5. *Arts*
6. Truffaut, 90
7. Truffaut, 20
8. Truffaut, 27
9. *McCall's*
10. Taylor, 65
11. Taylor, 101
12. Truffaut, 55
13. Spoto, 17
14. *McCall's*
15. Yacowar, 44
16. Truffaut, 55-6
17. *Picturegoer*
18. Truffaut, 59
19. *Cinema Quarterly*
20. Truffaut, 59

Chapter Six
1. *Picturegoer*, 1933
2. Spoto, 135
3. Truffaut, 70
4. *Hollywood Reporter*
5. Montagu, 239 footnote
6. December 13, 1934
7. Spoto, 144
8. *Stage*

9. Footnotes to the Film
10. Pudovkin, 24-5
11. Pudovkin, 168
12. Footnotes to the Film
13. *Cinema*

Chapter Seven
1. Footnotes to the Film, 1937
2. Montagu, 239 footnote
3. Auiler, 26-7
4. Footnotes to the Film
5. *McCall's*
6. *Stage*
7. Spoto, 170
8. PBS, November 1, 1999
9. *Encyclopaedia Britannica*
10. Footnotes to the Film
11. Truffaut, 76
12. Footnotes to the Film
13. *Listener*, March 10, 1937
14. *News Chronicle*
15. *Listener*, February 2, 1938
16. Leff, 18
17. *Film Weekly*
18. (Bogdanovich, 20)

Chapter 8
1. *World Film News*, 1938
2. *Encyclopaedia Britannica*
3. *World Film News*
4. *London Evening News*
5. Bogdanovich, 46
6. Truffaut, 241
7. Taylor, 95
8. Footnotes to the Film
9. *Film Weekly*
10. Ibid
11. *Rolling Stone*

12. *Film Weekly*
13. Footnotes to the Film
14. *Film Weekly*
15. Truffaut, 242
16. *Variety*
17. Truffaut, 149
18. Spoto, 110
19. Bogdanovich, 41
20. Taylor, 111
21. Samuels, 237
22. *Esquire*
23. Bogdanovich, 16
24. Truffaut, 189
25. Truffaut, 117-18
26. Truffaut, 36-7
27. Truffaut, 195
28. Truffaut, 178

FILMOGRAPHY

For most of the entries below, credits were transcribed from the films themselves, then supplemented by consulting Denis Gifford's *The British Film Catalogue, 1895-1985; A Reference Guide* (New York & Oxford: Facts on File, 1986), which lists the length of silent films in feet; David Quinlan's *British Sound Films; The Studio Years 1928-1959* (Totowa, N.J.: Barnes & Noble, 1984); Donald Spoto's *The Art of Alfred Hitchcock; Fifty Years of His Motion Pictures* (New York: Hopkinson and Blake, 1976); Robert A. Harris and Michael S. Lasky's *The Films of Alfred Hitchcock* (Secaucus, N.J.: The Citadel Press, 1976); and reviews in *Variety* and the *New York Times*.

Some inconsistencies have been left as they appear in the films' credits, so that photographer John J. Cox is also listed as Jack Cox and J.J. Cox. The misspelling of star Sylvia Sidney's name as "Sydney" on the opening credits of *Sabotage* has been corrected; otherwise, variations of names (of characters as well as cast and crew members) have been placed in brackets.

Exact running times are always problematic. When possible, I have timed a film myself and used that measurement, rounded off to the nearest minute. If a variant timing seems potentially valid (a cut version released in the United States, for example), it has been included in brackets. Silent films are a special challenge, for they were filmed and shown at a variety of speeds ranging from 16 to 24 frames per second. Features from the later 1920s tend to look best at 20-22 fps, but most videotape and DVD copies are recorded at the standard sound speed of 24 fps, which is usually too fast, or at 18 fps, which is definitely too slow. Here, I have listed the running time of the version I screened if the film appears complete and recorded at a relatively appropriate speed. Variant timings have been included in brackets.

Number Thirteen (1922) Unfinished short, 2 reels
CAST: Clare Greet; Ernest Thesiger

The Pleasure Garden (1926)
CREDITS: Scenario: Eliot Stannard; From the Novel by Oliver Sandys; Photography: Baron Ventimiglia; A Gainsborough-Emelka Production; Released by W & F; 7058 feet; 60 minutes [85]

CAST: Virginia Valli (Patsy Brand); Carmelita Geraghty (Jill Cheyne); Miles Mander (Levett); John Stuart (Hugh Fielding); Nita Naldi (Native Girl); George Schnell [Snell] (Oscar Hamilton); C. Falkenberg [Carl Falkenburg] (Prince Ivan); Ferdinand Martini [Frederic K. Martini] (Mr. Sidey); Florence Helminger (Mrs. Sidey)

The Mountain Eagle (1926; U.S.: *Fear O' God*)
CREDITS: Scenario: Eliot Stannard; From a Story by Charles Lapworth; Photography: Baron Ventimiglia; A Gainsborough-Emelka Production; Released by W & F; 7503 feet; 89 minutes

CAST: Nita Naldi (Beatrice); Malcolm Keen (Fear O' God Fulton); John Hamilton (Edward Pettigrew); Bernhard Goetzke (Mr. Pettigrew [Judge Pettigrew])

The Lodger: A Story of the London Fog (1926; U.S.: *The Case of Jonathan Drew*)
CREDITS: Scenario: Eliot Stannard; From the Novel by Mrs. Belloc Lowndes [Marie Belloc Lowndes]; Photography: Baron Ventimiglia; Art Direction: C. Wilfred Arnold, Bertram Evans; Editing and Titles: Ivor Montagu; Title Designs: E. McKnight Kauffer; Assistant Director: Alma Reville; A Gainsborough-Emelka Production; Released by W & F; 7500 feet; 89 minutes [67]

CAST: Marie Ault (The Landlady [Mrs. Bunting, Mrs. Jackson]); Arthur Chesney (Her Husband [Mr. Bunting, Mr. Jackson]); June [June Tripp] (Daisy, a mannequin [Daisy Bunting, Daisy Jackson]); Malcolm Keen (Joe, a police detective [Joe Chandler, Joe Betts]); Ivor Novello (The Lodger [Jonathan Drew])

Downhill (1927; U.S.: *When Boys Leave Home*)
CREDITS: Scenario: Eliot Stannard; from the Play by David LeStrange [Pseudonym of Ivor Novello and Constance Collier]; Photography: Claude McDonnell; Editing: Lionel Rich; Art Direction: Bert Evans; A Gainsborough Production; Released by W & F; 7600 feet; 95 minutes

CAST: Ivor Novello (Roddy Berwick); Isabel Jeans (Julia); Ian Hunter (Archie); Ben Webster (Dr. Dawson); Lilian Braithwaite (Lady Berwick); Norman McKinnel (Sir Thomas Berwick); Robin Irvine (Tim Walkeley [Wakeley]); Sybil Rhoda (Sybil Walkeley [Wakeley]); Annette Benson (Mabel); Alf Goddard (The Swede); Jerrold Robertshaw (Rev. Henry Walkeley [Wakeley]); Violet Farebrother (The Poetess); Barbara Gott (Mme. Michet); Hannah Jones (The Dressmaker)

Easy Virtue (1927)
CREDITS: Scenario: Eliot Stannard; From the Play by Noel Coward; Photography: Claude McDonnell; Art Direction: Clifford Pember; A Gainsborough Production; Presented by C.M. Woolf and Michael Balcon; Released by W & F; 7392 feet; 80 minutes [60]

CAST: Isabel Jeans (Larita Filton); Franklin Dyall (Her Husband); Eric Bransby Williams (The Co-respondent); Ian Hunter (The Plaintiff's Counsel); Robin Irvine (John Whittaker); Violet Farebrother (His Mother); Frank Elliott (His Father); Dacia Deane (His Elder Sister); Dorothy Boyd (His Younger Sister); Enid Stamp Taylor (Sarah); Benita Hume (Telephone Operator)

The Ring (1927)
CREDITS: Scenario: Alfred Hitchcock; Photography: John J. Cox; Art Direction: C.W. Arnold; A British International Production; Released by Wardour Films; 8454 feet; 89 minutes [100]

CAST: Carl Brisson ("One-Round" Jack Sander); Lilian Hall Davis [Lillian Hall-Davies] (The Girl); Ian Hunter (Bob Corby); Forrester Harvey (The Promoter); Harry Terry (The Showman); Gordon Harker (Jack's Trainer); Bdr. Billy Wells (Boxer); Charles Farrell (Second); Clare Greet (Gypsy [Fortune Teller])

The Farmer's Wife (1928)
CREDITS: Adaptation: Eliot Stannard; From the Play by Eden Phillpots; Photography: John J. Cox; Art Direction: C. Wilfred Arnold; A British International Production; Released by Wardour Films; 8875 feet; 97 minutes [67 / 129]

CAST: Jameson Thomas (Farmer Samuel Sweetland); Lilian Hall Davis [Lillian Hall-Davies] (Araminta Dench, his housekeeper); Gordon Harker (Churdles Ash, his handyman); Gibb McLaughlin (Henry Coaker); Maud Gill (Thirza Tapper); Louise Pounds (Widow Louisa Windeatt); Olga Slade (Mary Hearn, the postmistress); Ruth Maitland (Mercy Bassett, at the pub); Antonia Brough (Susan); Haward Watts (Dick Coaker); Mollie Ellis (Sibley Sweetland)

Champagne (1928)
CREDITS: Scenario: Eliot Stannard; Adaptation: Alfred Hitchcock; From an Original Story by Walter C. Mycroft; Photography: John J. Cox; Art Direction: C.W. Arnold; A British International Production; Released by Wardour Films; 8038 feet; 85 minutes

CAST: Betty Balfour (The Girl [Betty]); Jean Bradin (The Boy); Theo Von Alten (The Man); Gordon Harker (The Father); Clifford Heatherley (The Manager); Jack Trevor (The Officer); Sunday Wilshin (A Girl); Claude Hulbert (A Guest); Balliol & Merton (Dancers); Marcel Vibert (Maitre d'Hotel)

The Manxman (1929)
CREDITS: Scenario: Eliot Stannard; From the Novel by Sir Hall Caine; Photography: Jack Cox; Art Direction: C. W. Arnold; Editing: Emile de Ruelle; A British International Production; Released by Wardour Films; 8163 feet; 80 minutes [98 / 110]

CAST: Carl Brisson (Pete Quilliam); Malcolm Keen (Philip Christian); Anny Ondra (Kate Cregeen); Randle Ayrton (Caesar Cregeen); Claire Greet (Mrs. Cregeen); Wilfred Shine (Doctor); Kim Peacock (Ross Christian); Harry Terry (Man); Nellie Richards (Wardress)

Blackmail (1929)
CREDITS: Adaptation: Alfred Hitchcock; Dialogue: Benn Levy; From the Play by Charles Bennett; Photography: Jack Cox; Art Direction: C.W. Arnold; Editing: Emile de Ruelle; Musical Score by Campbell & Connelly; Compiled and Arranged by Hubert Bath, Harry Stafford; Conductor: John Reynders; A British International Production; Released by Wardour Films; 85 minutes [96]

CAST: Anny Ondra [with Joan Barry's voice] (Alice White); Sara Allgood (Mrs. White); Charles Paton (Mr. White); John Longden (Detective Frank Webber); Donald

Calthrop (Tracy); Cyril Ritchard (The Artist); Hannah Jones (The Landlady); Harvey Braban (The Chief Inspector); Ex-Detective Sergeant Bishop (The Detective Sergeant); Phyllis Monkman (The Neighbor); Percy Parsons (Crook); Johnny Butt (Sergeant)

Juno and the Paycock (1929; U.S.: *The Shame of Mary Boyle*)
CREDITS: Screenplay: Alma Reville; Adaptation: Alfred Hitchcock; From the Play by Sean O'Casey; Photography: J.J. Cox; Art Direction: J. Marchant; Editing: Emile de Ruelle; Sound Recording: C. Thornton; A British International Production; Released by Wardour Films; 94 minutes [85 / 99]

CAST: Sara Allgood (Mrs. Boyle ["Juno"]); Edward Chapman (Captain Jack Boyle); Sidney Morgan ("Joxer" Daly); John Longden (Charles Bentham); Kathleen O'Regan (Mary Boyle); John Laurie (Johnny Boyle); Donald Calthrop (Needle Nugent); Maire O'Neil (Mrs. Madigan); Dave Morris (Jerry Devine); Fred Schwarz (Mr. Kelly); Denis Wyndham (The Mobiliser); Barry Fitzgerald (The Orator)

Elstree Calling (1930)
CREDITS: Director: Adrian Brunel; Sketches and other interpolated items by Alfred Hitchcock; Ensemble Numbers Staged by Jack Hulbert, Paul Murray, Andre Charlot; Screenplay: Val Valentine; Photography: Claude Friese-Greene (some scenes in color); Editing: A.C. Hammond, under the supervision of Emile de Ruelle; Music: Reg Casson, Vivian Ellis, Chick Endor, Ivor Novello, Jack Strachey; Lyrics: Douglas Furber, Rowland Leigh, Donovan Parsons; Music Conductors: Teddy Brown, Sydney Baynes, John Reynders; Sound Recording: Alec Murray; A British International Production; Released by Wardour Films; 86 minutes

CAST: Tommy Handley (Announcer); Will Fyffe; Cicely Courtneidge; Jack Hulbert; Lily Morris; Helen Burnell; The Berkoffs; Bobby Comber; Lawrence Green; Ivor McLaren; Anna May Wong; Jameson Thomas; John Longden; Donald Calthrop; Gordon Harker; Hannah Jones; Little Teddy Brown and His Band; The Three Eddies; The Balalaika Choral Orchestra; The Adelpi Girls; The Charlot Girls

Murder! (1930)
CREDITS: Scenario: Alma Reville; Adaptation: Alfred Hitchcock, Walter Mycroft; From the Novel and Play *Enter Sir John*, by Clemence Dane and Helen Simpson; Photography: J.J. Cox; Art Direction: J.F. Mead; Editing: Rene Marrison, under the supervision of Emile de Ruelle; Musical Direction: John Reynders; Sound Recording: Cecil V. Thornton; A British International Production; Released by Wardour Films; 103 minutes [92 / 108]

CAST: Herbert Marshall (Sir John Menier); Norah Baring (Diana Baring); Phyllis Konstam (Doucie Markham); Edward Chapman (Ted Markham); Miles Mander (Gordon Druce); Esme Percy (Handel Fane); Donald Calthrop (Ion Stewart); Esme V. Chaplin (Prosecuting Counsel); Amy Brandon-Thomas (Defending Counsel); Joynson Powell (Judge); S.J. Warmington (Bennett); Marie Wright (Miss Mitcham); Hannah Jones (Mrs. Didsome); Una O'Connor (Mrs. Grogram); R.E. Jeffrey (Jury Foreman);

Alan Stainer, Kenneth Kove, Guy Pelham Boulton, Violet Farebrother, Clare Greet, Drusilla Wills, Robert Easton, William Fazan, George Smythson, Ross Jefferson, Picton Roxborough (Jurors); Gus McNaughton (Tom Trewitt)

Hitchcock also directed a German-language version of *Murder!*, entitled *Mary* (*Sir John greift ein!*). Screenplay: Alma Reville, Herbert Juttke, Dr. Georg C. Klaren. Cast: Alfred Abel; Olga Tschechowa; Paul Graetz; Lotte Stein; Ekkehard Arendt; Jack Mylong-Münz; Louis Ralph; Hermine Sterler; Fritz Alberti; Hertha V. Walther

The Skin Game (1931)
CREDITS: Scenario: Alma Reville; Adaptation: Alfred Hitchcock; From the Play by John Galsworthy; Photography: J.J. Cox; Art Direction: J.B. Maxwell; Editing: A. Gobbett, R. Marrison; Sound Recording: Alec Murray; A British International Production; Released by Wardour Films; 82 minutes [79 / 88]

CAST: C.V. France (Mr. Hillcrist); Helen Haye (Mrs. Hillcrist); Jill Esmond (Jill Hillcrist); Edmund Gwenn (Mr. Hornblower); John Longden (Charles Hornblower); Phyllis Konstam (Chloe Hornblower); Frank Lawton (Rolf Hornblower); Herbert Ross, Dora Gregory (The Jackmans); Edward Chapman (Dawker); R.E. Jeffrey (First Stranger); George Bancroft (Second Stranger); Ronald Frankau (Auctioneer)

Number Seventeen (1932)
CREDITS: Producer: John Maxwell; Scenario: Alma Reville, Alfred Hitchcock, Rodney Ackland; From the Play *Number Seventeen* by J. Jefferson Farjeon, Produced by Leon M. Lion; Photography: John J. Cox, Byran Langley; Art Direction: Wilfred Arnold; Film and Sound Editing: A.C. Hammond; Musical Score: A. Hallis; Sound Recording: A.D. Valentine; A British International Production; Released by Wardour Films Ltd.; 62 minutes [66]

CAST: Leon M. Lion (Ben); Anne Grey (The Girl [Nora Brant]); John Stuart (The Detective [Gilbert Fordyce; Detective Barton]); Donald Calthrop (Brant); Barry Jones (Henry Doyle); Ann Casson (Rose Ackroyd); Henry Caine (Ackroyd); Garry Marsh (Sheldrake); Herbert Langley (Guard)

Rich and Strange (1932; U.S.: *East of Shanghai*)
CREDITS: Scenario: Alma Reville, Val Valentine; Adaptation: Alfred Hitchcock; From an Unspecified Work by Dale Collins; Photography: John Cox, Charles Martin; Art Direction: C. Wilfred Arnold; Editing: Rene Marrison, Winifred Cooper; Music: Hal Dolphe; Musical Direction: John Reynders; Sound Recording: Alec Murray; A British International Production; Released by Wardour Films Ltd.; 83 minutes [92 / 95]

CAST: Henry Kendall (Fred Hill); Joan Barry (Emily Hill); Percy Marmont (Commander Gordon); Betty Amann (The Princess); Elsie Randolph (Miss Imery); Hannah Jones (Mrs. Porter); Aubrey Dexter (The Colonel)

Waltzes from Vienna (1933; U.S.: *Strauss's Great Waltz*)
CREDITS: Producer: Tom Arnold; Scenario: Alma Reville, Guy Bolton; From the Play *The Great Waltz [Walzerkreig]* by Heinz Reichert, Dr. A.M. Willner, Ernst Marischka; Photography: Glen MacWilliams; Art Direction: Alfred Junge; Editing: Charles Frend; Music: Johann Strauss, Sr. & Jr., adapted by Hubert Bath; Musical Direction: Louis Levy; A Tom Arnold Production; Released by Gaumont British; 81 minutes

CAST: Jessie Matthews (Rasi); Edmund Gwenn (Johann Strauss, the elder); Fay Compton (The Countess [Countess Helga von Stahl]); Esmond Knight (Johann Strauss, the younger [Schani Strauss]); Frank Vosper (The Prince [Count Gustav von Stahl]); Robert Hale (Ebezeder); Charles Heslop (Crump [The Valet]); Hindle Edgar (Leopold); Marcus Barron (Anton Drexter); Betty Huntley Wright (The Maid); Sybil Grove (Mme. Fouchet); Cyril Smith (The Secretary); Bill Shine [Billy Shine, Jr.] (The Cook [Carl]); Bertram Dench (The Engine Driver); B.M. Lewin [Lewis] (Domeyer); Berinoff & Charlot

The Man Who Knew Too Much (1934)
CREDITS: Associate Producer: Ivor Montagu; Scenario: Edwin Greenwood, A.R. Rawlinson; Additional Dialogue: Emlyn Williams; From a Story by Charles Bennett, D.B. Wyndham Lewis; Photography: Curt Courant; Art Direction: Alfred Junge; Editing: H. St. C. Stewart; Music: Arthur Benjamin; Musical Direction: Louis Levy; Sound Recording: F. McNally; A Gaumont-British Production; Released by General Film Distributors; 80 minutes [75]

CAST: Leslie Banks (Bob Lawrence); Edna Best (Jill Lawrence); Peter Lorre (Abbott); Frank Vosper (Ramon); Hugh Wakefield (Uncle Clive); Nova Pilbeam (Betty Lawrence); Pierre Fresnay (Louis Bernard); Cicely Oates (Nurse Agnes); D.A. Clarke Smith (Inspector Binstead); George Curzon (Gibson); Henry Oscar (George Barbor)

The 39 Steps (1935)
CREDITS: Dialogue: Ian Hay; Continuity: Alma Reville; Adaptation: Charles Bennett; From the Novel by John Buchan; Photography: Bernard Knowles; Art Direction: O. Werndorff; Dress Design: J. Strassner; Wardrobe: Marianne; Editing: D.N. Twist; Musical Direction: Louis Levy; Sound Recording: A. Birck; A Gaumont-British Production; Released by General Film Distributors; 86 minutes [83]

CAST: Robert Donat (Richard Hannay); Madeleine Carroll (Pamela); Lucie Mannheim (Miss Smith); Godfrey Tearle (Professor Jordan); Peggy Ashcroft (The Crofter's Wife [Margaret]); John Laurie (The Crofter [John]); Helen Haye (Mrs. Jordan [Louisa]); Frank Cellier (The Sheriff); Wylie Watson (Mr. Memory); Gus MacNaughton, Jerry Verno (Commercial Travellers); Peggy Simpson (The Maid); Hilda Trevelyan (The Innkeeper's Wife); John Turnbull (Inspector); Frederick Piper

Secret Agent (1936)
CREDITS: Screenplay: Charles Bennett; Dialogue: Ian Hay; Additional Dialogue: Jesse Lasky, Jr.; Continuity: Alma Reville; From the Play by Campbell Dixon; Based

BIBLIOGRAPHY

Sources Cited:

Auiler, Dan. *Hitchcock's Notebooks: An Authorized and Illustrated Look Inside the Creative Mind of Alfred Hitchcock.* New York: Spike, An Avon Book, 1999.

Balcon, Michael. *Michael Balcon Presents . . . A Lifetime of Films.* London: Hutchinson, 1969.

Bogdanovich, Peter. *The Cinema of Alfred Hitchcock.* New York: Museum of Modern Art Film Library, 1963.

Freeman, David. "The Last Days of Alfred Hitchcock." *Esquire*, April 1982, 81-101, 105.

Gottlieb, Sidney (editor). *Hitchcock on Hitchcock: Selected Writings and Interviews.* Berkeley, Los Angeles, and London: University of California, 1995.

Hitchcock, Alfred. "Are Stars Necessary?" *Picturegoer*, December 16, 1933 (essay reprinted in Gottlieb, 76-78).

_____"Close Your Eyes and Visualize!" *Stage*, July 1936 (essay reprinted in Gottlieb, 246-49).

_____Lecture delivered at Columbia University on March 30, 1939 (typescript published in Gottlieb, 267-74).

_____"Direction." In *Footnotes to the Film*, edited by Charles Davy. New York: Oxford University Press, 1937 (essay reprinted in Gottlieb, 253-61).

_____"Director's Problems." *The Listener*, February 2, 1938 (essay reprinted in Gottlieb, 186-91).

_____"Film Production." *Encyclopedia Britannica*, Vol. 15, 1965 edition, under the general heading, "Motion Pictures" (essay reprinted in Gottlieb, 210-26).

_____"Films We Could Make." *London Evening News*, November 16, 1927 (essay reprinted in Gottlieb, 165-67).

_____"How I Choose My Heroines." In *Who's Who in Filmland*, edited by Langford Reed and Hetty Spiers. London: Chapman and Hall, 1931 (essay reprinted in Gottlieb, 73-75).

_____"If I Were Head of a Production Company." *Picturegoer*, January 26, 1935 (essay reprinted in Gottlieb, 172-75).

_____"Let 'Em Play God." *Hollywood Reporter* 100, No. 47, October 11, 1948 (essay reprinted in Gottlieb, 113-15).

_____"Life Among the Stars." *News Chronicle*, March 1-5, 1937 (essay reprinted in Gottlieb, 27-50).

_____"Much Ado About Nothing?" *The Listener*, March 10, 1937 (essay reprinted in Gottlieb, 179-82).

_____"Why I Am Afraid of the Dark." ("Pourquoi J'ai Peur la Nuit") *Arts: Lettres, Spectacles* 777, June 1-7, 1960 (essay translated by Claire Marrone and published in Gottlieb, 142-45).

_____"The Woman Who Knows Too Much." *McCall's* #83, March 1956 (essay reprinted in Gottlieb, 51-53).

Hodenfield, Chris. "Muuuurder by the Babbling Brook." *Rolling Stone*, July 29, 1976, 38-43, 56.

Leff, Leonard J. *Hitchcock and Selznick; the Rich and Strange Collaboration of Al fred Hitchcock and David O. Selznick in Hollywood*. New York: Weidenfeld & Nicolson, 1987.

Martin, Pete. "I Call on Alfred Hitchcock." *Saturday Evening Post*, July 27, 1957. In *Film Makers on Film Making*, edited by Harry M. Geduld. Bloomington and London: Indiana University, 1967, 123-34.

Montagu, Ivor. *Film World*. Baltimore: Penguin, 1964.

Murf. "'Menace Must Have True Foundation.'" *Variety*, January 17, 1973, 2, 68.

"On Style." *Cinema* 1, no. 5, August-September 1963 (Hitchcock interview reprinted in Gottlieb, 285-302).

Perkoff, Leslie. "The Censor and Sydney Street." *World Film News* 2, no. 12, March 1938 (Hitchcock interview reprinted in Gottlieb, 192-95).

Pudovkin, V.I. "Introduction to the German Edition." In *Film Technique and Film Acting*. New York: Grove, 1960, 23-28. (This introduction to *Filmregie und Filmmanuskript*, translated by Georg and Nadia Friedland, was re-translated from German to English by Ivor Montagu and first published in *The Film Weekly*, London, October 29, 1928.)

_____"Types Instead of Actors." In *Film Technique and Film Acting*. New York: Grove, 1960, 165-73. (This chapter is the text of a lecture delivered to the Film Society, London, on February 3, 1929 by Pudovkin, who used this English translation by Ivor Montagu and S.S.N., which was published, with slight changes, in *Cinema*, February 6, 1929.)

Samuels, Charles Thomas. *Encountering Directors*. New York: G.P. Putnam's Sons, 1972.

Schickel, Richard. *The Men Who Made the Movies*. New York: Atheneum, 1975.

Taylor, John Russell. *Hitch: The Life & Times of Alfred Hitchcock*. New York: Berkley, 1980 (Paperback edition of the 1978 biography.)

Truffaut, François. *Hitchcock*. New York: Simon and Schuster, 1967 (interviews conducted in 1962).

Spoto, Donald. *The Dark Side of Genius*. Boston and Toronto: Little, Brown and Company, 1983.

Watts, Stephen. "On Music in Films." *Cinema Quarterly* (Edinburgh) 2, no. 2, Winter 1933-34 (Hitchcock interview reprinted in Gottlieb, 241-45).

Williams, J. Danvers. "The Censor Wouldn't Pass It." *Film Weekly*, November 5, 1938 (Hitchcock interview reprinted in Gottlieb, 196-201).

Yacowar, Maurice. *Hitchcock's British Films*. Hamden, Connecticut: Archon, 1977.

Other Sources:

Buchan, John. *The 39 Steps*. New York: Popular Library, n.d.

Conrad, Joseph. *The Secret Agent*. Garden City: Doubleday Anchor Books, 1953.

Du Maurier, Daphne. *Jamaica Inn*. New York: Triangle Books, 1941.

Maugham, W. Somerset. *Ashenden: The British Agent*. Harmondsworth, England, et al.: Penguin Books, 1977.

Tey, Josephine. *A Shilling for Candles*. New York: The Macmillan Company, 1954.

White, Ethel Lina. *The Lady Vanishes*. New York: Zebra Books, 1987. (Reprint of *The Wheel Spins* under the film's title.)

(Photofest)

INDEX

Numbers in boldface indicate illustrations.

ABOUT THE AUTHOR

Paul M. Jensen is a Professor at the State University of New York at Oneonta. A member of the Communications Arts Department, he teaches courses in film history, appreciation and production. After graduating from SUNY—Albany, Mr. Jensen received his M.F.A. in Film, Radio and Television from Columbia University. He is the author of four books—*The Cinema of Fritz Lang* (1969), *Boris Karloff and His Films* (1974), *The Men Who Made the Monsters* (1996) and *Hitchcock Becomes "HITCHCOCK"* and has published articles on film-related subjects in various periodicals, including *Film Comment*, *Films in Review*, *Midnight Marquee*, *Scarlet Street*, *Variety* and *Video Watchdog*.